D1103843

LEARNING TO LOVE

WHEN LOVE ISN'T EASY

DAVID WALLS

VICTOR BOOKS

A DIVISION OF SCRIPTURE PRESS PUBLICATIONS INC.
USA CANADA ENGLAND

Copyediting: Carole Streeter, Barbara Williams
Cover Design: Scott Rattray
Cover Illustration: Robert Bergin

Library of Congress Cataloging-in-Publication Data

Walls, David R.
  Learning to love when love isn't easy / by David Walls.
      p.   cm.
  Includes bibliographical references.
  ISBN 0-89693-909-X
  1. Christian life — 1960-   2. Love — Religious aspects — Christianity.
3. Interpersonal relations — Religious aspects — Christianity. I. Title.
BV4501.2.W324   1992
241'.4 — dc20   92-6254
                                                                              CIP

1   2   3   4   5   6   7   8   9   10   Printing/Year   96   95   94   93   92

Contents

Dedication

Every so often the Lord allows certain people to intersect your life, and in that moment of time there results a lifetime of benefit. Although I am confident that I am not alone in this sentiment, as I look back over my years of ministry, I am thankful that it is true.

Over the last twenty years God has strategically placed in my path five people of special note. If it were not for this quintet of influence, I would not have written this book. In fact, I imagine that I may not have even pursued, for any length of time, the pastoral ministry. Each, in his own unique way, has placed his mark on me and I am the better for it.

So it is with deep respect, gratitude, and love that I dedicate this book to:

—**Chuck Swindoll** . . . who has modeled ministry and preaching for me, up close and from a distance. Who has unselfishly given of his time to counsel and confront me when I needed it the most. Whose laughter and joy still echo in my heart. I shall be always grateful for his continuing imprint on my life. Thank you!

—**Kent Hughes** . . . who has stood alongside me since my earliest days at seminary. Who continues to see potential in what I do. Who has modeled constancy and faithfulness throughout his ministry . . . characteristics that I trust will also mark me. Thank you!

—**Arnold McNeill** . . . my father-in-law . . . whose influence began even farther back . . . whose wisdom in ministry remains a source of strength for me . . . whose family stands tall as a testimony to that wisdom . . . and whose loyalty and friendship have helped me survive when surviving was questionable. Thank you!

—**Kent and Jeremy Walls** . . . my sons and two of my best "buds," as they would say. They continue to cheer me on as their dad. They amaze me with their insight into God's Word and His world. Their faith excites me and challenges me also. They have taught me a great deal about learning to love. I am proud to be on their team. Thank you!

To these five I again say thank you. Thank you for making my life richer and fuller. God has been so good to me . . . to include you in my journey.

I would be remiss if I did not also thank my wife and best friend, Patricia. This book represents the both of us. Her unwavering love for me has encouraged and pushed me to love when love isn't easy. Thank you, Patricia.

Foreword

We live in a fast-paced and deliberate age. We eat prepro-cessed meals that taste great but often have forgotten to include nutrients in the midst of all the chemicals to stimu-late our taste buds. We outfit our leisure with high-tech, neon equipment that lets us go higher and farther, but somehow has lost the concept that leisure includes relax-ation. And, we have programmed relationships that keep us in a frenzy on the activity circuit, swirling in a network of many friendships, but too often lack the crucial element of love.

It is in this vacuum that Dr. David Walls writes *Learning to Love When Love Isn't Easy*. This is not a book by a prophet, though he challenges us not to forget the most important aspect of our relationships. This is not a theologi-cal treatise, though it is deeply founded in the impeccable biblical scholarship for which Dr. David Walls is known. This is not just a shallow collection of stories that will pull the heartstrings, though it is amply illustrated with power-ful examples that drive each point home in a visual and clear manner.

Learning to Love When Love Isn't Easy is a book that reminds, challenges, teaches, and provides hope that love can be a natural part of our friendships. It is returning the lost element that forms the centerpiece of purpose and goal of every Christlike relationship. I hope you enjoy reading this solid book, with a powerful message, written in a relevant style.

Howard G. Hendricks
Chairman, Center for Christian Leadership
Distinguished Professor, Dallas Theological Seminary

1
THE MISSING
INGREDIENT

*If I speak with the tongues of men and of angels,
but do not have love, I have become a noisy gong
or a clanging cymbal. And if I have the gift of
prophecy, and know all mysteries and
all knowledge; and if I have all faith,
so as to remove mountains, but do not have love,
I am nothing. And if I give all my possessions
to feed the poor, and if I deliver my body
to be burned, but do not have love,
it profits me nothing.*

*Love is patient, love is kind, and is not jealous;
love does not brag and is not arrogant, does not
act unbecomingly; it does not seek its own,
is not provoked, does not take into account
a wrong suffered, does not rejoice
in unrighteousness, but rejoices with the truth;
bears all things, believes all things,
hopes all things, endures all things.*

*Love never fails, but if there are gifts of prophecy,
they will be done away; if there are tongues,
they will cease, if there is knowledge,
it will be done away. For we know in part,
and we prophesy in part; but when the perfect
comes, the partial will be done away.*

When I was a child, I used to speak as a child,
think as a child, reason as a child; when I became
a man, I did away with childish things.
For now we see in a mirror dimly, but then
face to face; now I know in part, but then I shall
know fully just as I also have been fully known.
But now abide faith, hope, love, these three,
but the greatest of these is love.

1 Corinthians 13

Maybe you saw it. If you did, you probably will not forget it. The program was "Highway to Heaven" and the angel was Michael Landon. That particular evening, my two young sons and I curled up together on the recliner to watch the program.

The story focused on a retarded boy named Arnie who was nine or ten years of age. He had left home because his father laughed at him, beat him, and said that he talked funny. And Arnie did. His mouth hung crooked on one side, and he could not form his words well. So he stumbled and slurred his speech regularly. His father was not impressed and so Arnie left home and lived in an alley in a large box, with his best friend, a cat named Thomas.

The scene that caught my heart was when Arnie shoplifted some cat food for Thomas and some candles for himself. You see, it was his birthday and he wanted to celebrate it with his best friend. He opened the cat food tin, placed the candles on top, and lit all of them. Then he closed his eyes and before he blew them out he made a wish: "I wish that somebody would love me."

You may also recall from your childhood the familiar tale, *The Wizard of Oz*. In that story there is a conversation between the scarecrow and the tin woodman. "I don't know enough," said the scarecrow cheerfully. "My head is stuffed with straw, you know, and that is why I'm going to Oz, to ask him for some brains."

"Oh, I see," said the tin woodman. "But after all, brains are not the best things in the world."

"Have you any?" inquired the scarecrow.

"No, my head is quite empty," answered the tin woodman, "but once I had brains and a heart also. Having tried them both, *I should much rather have a heart.*"

I want to talk to you about the heart — the missing ingredient in our relationships, whether in our homes, at work, or at church. As we slide into the long hot days of summer, or as we struggle through the icy deep of a frigid winter when tempers can flair and patience run thin, it is crucial for us to examine our own behavior under the banner of biblical love. On the surface your home may seem the epitome of wonderful. It can be running smoothly with little or no difficulty; but if it is not being fueled and nurtured by love, something is seriously missing. A church can have the finest programming, the sharpest buildings, and a school and bookstore second to none; but all of that means absolutely nothing if true biblical love is missing. Before we assume that we practice biblical love, it is important to understand precisely what love is.

THE IMPORTANCE OF LOVE

Paul, the apostle of first-century vintage, understood it. In one of the most familiar sections of the Bible he involved his readers in an extended discourse on the subject. In 1 Corinthians 13, he introduced the subject by extolling the importance of love.

> If I speak with the tongues of men and of angels but do not have love, I have become a noisy gong or a clanging cymbal. And if I have the gift of prophecy, and know all mysteries and all knowledge, and if I have all faith, so as

to remove mountains, but do not have love, I am nothing. And if I give all my possessions to feed the poor, and if I deliver my body to be burned, but do not have love, it profits me nothing (vv. 1-3).

The thrust of these verses is that love is the essential ingredient in everything that we do. Without it, our sincere and impressive deeds amount to nothing. Dr. D.A. Carson, Professor of New Testament at Trinity Evangelical Divinity School, comments on these verses:

> If Paul were addressing the modern church today perhaps he would say this, "You Christians, who prove your spirituality by the amount of theological information you can cram into your heads, I tell you that such knowledge by itself proves nothing. And you who affirm the Spirit's presence in your meetings because there is a certain style of worship, whether formal and stately or exuberant and spontaneous, if your worship patterns are not expressions of love, you are spiritually bankrupt. You who insist that speaking in tongues attests a second work of the Spirit, of baptism of the Spirit, I tell you that if love does not characterize your life, there is not evidence of even a first work of the Spirit."[1]

The reason that Paul the apostle can make such an exacting statement is because the love he is talking about is unique: it is a love born out of the heart of God. The word translated "love" throughout this chapter is the Greek word *agape*. Jesus said that if Christians evidenced this, people would be able to tell that they were related to Him. This work of love begins when we come to know Jesus Christ.

But agape love is very different than our normal concept of love. Agape love is volitional, not emotional; that is, agape love refers to our will. It is a decision we make, not a feeling we have. When we talk about falling in love, we're not talking about agape love. Over and over in the New Testament we read, "Love one another." This agape love can be commanded. We cannot command feelings, but we can command an active determination of our will. Having said that, let me remind you of some other factors inherent in the term *agape* that relate to our love for others.

• The *source* of agape love is not the character or the worth of the individual you are intending to love, or even their need. The source of agape love is the nature of the person who is loving. God loves us with agape love, not because of who or what we are, or even what we're going to become. He loves us because of who He is.

• The *goal* of agape love is the good of the other person. Agape love always seeks the highest good of the other person, whatever the cost. For God the Father, the cost was His Son, Jesus Christ.

• The *evidence* of agape love is action. Agape love does not simply feel or speak or even think. Rather, it chooses to act in the best interest of another person.

• The *extent* of agape love is sacrifice. Without sacrifice there is no love, for by its very nature, this love is outpouring, not self-seeking. Agape love does not act when it is convenient; it acts even though there is a cost.[2]

Furthermore, agape love does not make value judgments on the worth of the person before it determines to do something for that person. It doesn't say, "You are worth loving . . . but you are not."

Agape love simply gives without expecting any repayment. It goes the extra mile, in spite of the other person's faults. Agape love is a giving kind of love.

One of the finest definitions of this love I have ever seen comes from a very unexpected pen. Erich Fromm, well known in psychiatric circles and not thought to be a believer, defines agape love when he writes:

Love means to commit oneself without guarantee, to give oneself completely in the hope that our love will produce love in the loved person.

Love is an act of faith and whoever is of little faith is also of little love. The perfect love would be one that gives all and expects nothing. It would, of course, be willing and delighted to take anything that was offered, the more the better. But it would ask for nothing. For if one expects nothing and asks nothing, he can never be deceived or disappointed. It is only when love demands that it brings on pain.[3]

That's the kind of love that Paul is talking about, a love that is essential to everything we do. In the case of the Corinthian church, agape love was absolutely necessary for their health and unity, because this church was on the verge of disintegration. If you examine the previous chapters of 1 Corinthians, you will discover a litany of problems.

Chapter 1 discusses the disunity rampant within the church. Chapter 2 examines the criticisms people had of Paul's preaching. Chapter 3 emphasizes the jealousy and strife that existed in the church and declares that even though the people had all the spiritual gifts, they were fleshly because of their jealousy. Chapter 4 details their judgmental attitude toward one another. Chapter 5 condemns their tolerance of immorality and their lack of church discipline. Chapter 6 expresses horror that they took other believers to court and sued the pants off of them. The list goes on.

The principle of agape love is true today, in our homes and in our churches. A home that is struggling, that is seething with anger and division and friction and jealousy, can be turned around with the practice of agape love. The same is true in a church.

Amy Carmichael, a missionary to India for many years, reminds us of the importance of agape love in these words:

> If I belittle those whom I am called to serve, talk of their weak points, in contrast perhaps with what I think are my strong points, then I know nothing of Calvary love.
>
> If I take offense easily, if I am content to continue in cool unfriendliness, though friendship be possible, then I know nothing of Calvary love.
>
> If I feel bitter toward those who have condemned me, as it seems to me, unjustly, forgetting that if they knew me as I know myself they would condemn me much more, then I know nothing of Calvary love.[4]

THE QUALITIES OF LOVE

It is Calvary love, agape love, that Paul wants us to know about. That's why he doesn't stop by simply reminding us of the importance of love, but goes on to outline the basic qualities, the actions and the attitudes, that should characterize this kind of love in our churches and in our homes.

• Agape love is constructive. "Love is patient, love is kind . . . is not provoked" (vv. 4-5).

The constructiveness of agape love has two prongs, two aspects. First of all, *love is patient.* Our word for patience is a combination of two small Greek words that means "a long way from anger." That's what patience is. One problem all of us battle in our relationships is the short fuse. We blame it on schedules, on stress loads, on pressures; we can call it whatever we want, but the fact is that we have a short fuse. Something goes wrong and we fly off the handle. We can say the cruelest things in anger to those who are closest to us. Sometimes we discipline our children in anger, venting our frustration.

John Chrysostom, the golden-tongued preacher of the fourth century, described anger this way:

> Anger is a fire. It catches, destroys, and consumes. Let us quench it by long-suffering and patience. For as red hot iron dipped into water loses its fire, so an angry man falling in with a patient one does no harm to the patient man, but rather, benefits him and is himself more thoroughly cooled or subdued.[5]

The patience of agape love works against the short fuse. What that means in our relationships is that perhaps we must put up with some annoyances, some things that we don't particularly like. It means that we will accept the mistakes of the members of our family, of our church, without being bent out of shape. That's what Paul is getting at here in verse 5 when he says, "Love is not provoked." The word *provoke* means "to be irritated."

Think about the kinds of things that irritate you, that drive you crazy at home . . . like socks and underwear on the floor. You know your husband's up and gone to the office because he has left a trail to the garage. What about bicycles in the driveway? Or nylons hung over the shower rods? Or a husband who's always late for dinner and doesn't call?

What irritates you at church? The format of the bulletin? Too many choruses? Going charismatic? The length of the service? The color of the carpet? The teaching methods of your Sunday School teacher?

With agape love, we realize the difference between the things we should really be concerned about and the things we should forget about. But isn't it true that what really tees us off are the little things? In the light of eternity and, frankly, in the light of next Friday, they couldn't matter less. Agape love learns to ignore petty things and makes a conscious choice not to be angry about them but to be patient.

• Agape love is kind. The word *kind* comes from a term describing things that were pleasant, like good food, or clothing that was comfortable to wear. The application for us is that when we disagree with one another, we ought to weigh our words carefully, making sure that they are comfortable to wear, good to taste. Be kind. Two centuries ago the great revivalist, John Wesley, said it well:

> Let love not visit you as a transient guest, but be the constant (partner) of your soul. See that your heart is filled at all times . . . with real (undiluted) benevolence, not to those only who love you, but to every soul. Let it pant in your heart, let it sparkle in your eyes, let it shine in all your actions. Whenever you open your lips, let it be with love. And let there be on your tongue the law of kindness . . .[6]

• Agape love is satisfied or content. "Love is not jealous, love does not brag, and is not arrogant." The word *jealous* has an interesting history. The Hebrews, in fact, used only one word for jealousy in the Old Testament; it meant "to be intensely red in the face," and described one whose face flushed as a sudden flow of blood announced a surge of emotion.

In the New Testament, *jealousy* comes from a word that means "to boil over with emotion." And so we start to get a picture of jealousy as a feeling of discontent or resentment because someone has something that we want.

Recently, two professors of psychology at Yale University reported in *Psychology Today* their study of jealousy. They concluded that jealousy is rooted in low self-esteem or insecurities about self-worth. People who tend to jealousy also tend to have three personality characteristics. First, they have a low opinion of themselves. Second, they see a large discrepancy between how they really are and what they would ideally like to be. Third, they value highly such visible achievements as being wealthy, famous, well-liked and, especially, physically attractive.[7]

Believers who operate with agape love resist that tug because they are satisfied with who they are and what they have. They have biblical self-worth because they understand their position in Jesus Christ. They want to mature and grow, but they are not so dissatisfied by where they are in comparison with someone else that it is a handicap to them.

They see their role in life as valuable. They understand their place. It drives me crazy when someone asks a mother who stays at home with her children, "Do you work?" and the answer she gives is, "No, I don't." I've tried to take care of the house and kids for three hours when my wife is gone, and I'm a basket case when she comes back. I need to go golfing just to get my sanity back together. A housewife who works at home *works* at home. Hers is a valuable role, an important contribution.

People who are content understand their place in ministry. "Well, I'm only a nursery worker here." What do you mean you're *only* a nursery worker? You are a *nursery worker* and you have an important function.

Additionally, contented people are thankful for whatever God has graciously provided in their lives in terms of material possessions. They are not jealously looking over everyone else's shoulder for their position, their place, their providence, their power.

• Agape love is not proud. Paul uses two words to stress his point in verse 4. He talks about love not bragging and not being arrogant. The Greek verb for *to brag* means "to be a windbag." It refers to outward display of pride where you continually remind your family and friends how important you are. This kind of display is evidence of a person who is not content or satisfied but must have the attention of others. The word *arrogant* is different. It refers not to an outward display, but to an inner attitude or disposition. You may not display pride on the outside, but internally you view yourself as superior to others. You chafe because your opinion is not sought, because your advice or point of view is not acted upon immediately, or even agreed with. Agape love is not concerned about that because it is a decision, an act of the will that directs its attention to others, not to itself.

• Agape love does not act unbecomingly or rudely. It does not seek its own. "Love is not selfish," Paul said. The verb for *to seek* is an intense word meaning "to demand or to require." It conveys the idea of striving for your own advantage, of working hard to have your way all of the time.

Does that describe you? Things must go your way, regardless? A home, a family, a marriage, a church that is operating with that mind-set has lost the concept of agape love, of servanthood, of being able to assist one another, of looking out for the best interest of another. And yet a most common phenomena in the church is conflict in which one side will not budge, or in marriage where one marriage partner will not apologize.

Stubborn and willful marriage partners can cause unhappiness to everyone in the home. Their self-will seldom, if ever, gives in to those around them. With mulelike obstinacy, they keep demanding their own way and looking for every possible means and method of doing or having what they want. They will not listen to reason; they will not consider the feelings of others; they will not face up to the potential consequences of their actions. They believe they are right and others are wrong, and they are determined to have their own way. Such people know absolutely nothing about agape love. They know only self-love.

Dr. Harry Stack Sullivan has said it well, "When the satisfaction, security, and development of another person becomes as significant to you as your own satisfaction, security, and development, *love exists.*"[8] That's because selfishness does not.

Oliver Cromwell, the brilliant leader of England during the seventeenth century, once decreed that a young man would be executed at the ringing of curfew. The young man's fiancée came to Cromwell and pleaded for his life, but Cromwell would not listen. "The young man you love will die at the ringing of curfew," he said. The old and very deaf sexton went to the church that night to ring curfew. Unknown to him, the girl who loved that young man had climbed up inside that great bell and was hanging on for dear life to the clapper so that every time the sexton pulled the bell rope, thinking it was ringing loud and clear, her body was hitting against one side of the bell and then another without a note being struck. When he finished what he thought was the ringing of the curfew, the girl made her way down, battered, bloody, bruised. And as she came stumbling down the hill, Oliver Cromwell was already on his way up to find out why the curfew had not rung when suddenly he saw her. Looking her in the eye, recognizing what she had done, he said, "Curfew shall not ring tonight."

Her pleas had not moved him; her arguments had not moved him; but her love he understood. It was unselfish love.

• Agape love is forgiving. The end of verse 5 and the first part of verse 7 help us here. Love "does not take into account a wrong suffered. . . . Love bears all things." I want you to consider that phrase, "take into account." The words literally mean "to let your mind dwell on something or to hold something against someone and to punish them for it." We tend to do that, don't we? We like to keep scores and stakes. We can come to church with a scorecard in our hands, just waiting for something to go wrong so that we can make a note of it.

We also like to keep scores in our relationships. Every time a crisis comes along with another person, we hash over the past and resurrect old feelings and actions that should have been done long ago. I am so glad that my God does not treat me in that way. In 2 Corinthians 5 we read:

> Therefore if any man is in Christ, he is a new creature; the old things passed away; behold, new things have come. Now, all these things are from God, who reconciled us to Himself through Christ, and gave us the ministry of reconciliation, namely, that God was in Christ reconciling the world to Himself, not counting their trespasses against them (vv. 17-19).

The words "not counting" are from the same Greek words translated as "does not take into account," in 1 Corinthians 13:5, "not keeping score." And don't pass over the word "trespasses" because it has an interesting meaning. It refers simply to mistakes. It is not the usual word for sin, but refers to a person who was writing a letter and made a spelling error—little things. This verse is saying that God does not let His mind dwell on our small mistakes. He doesn't let His mind dwell on anything that we do that is wrong or sinful; the emphasis here is particularly on the small things, because that is where we have the most trouble. We like to keep track, to keep score of the little errors. Agape love forgives.

• Agape love bears all things. That means it is a love that protects by covering or by keeping secret. In other words, love hides, it excuses the errors and the faults of others. We're not talking here of a lifestyle of sin where confrontation and discipline must occur. We're talking about everyday slipups.

One man translated verse 7 this way, "Love throws a cloak of silence over what is displeasing in another person." Do you do that? Do you throw a cloak of silence over what is displeasing in your husband, your wife, your children, your pastors, your fellow Christians at the church?

Or do you dwell on it, camp on it? Do you continually remind your spouse, children, friends, about their past mistakes or errors that you have kept score of so diligently? That is not what agape love would do.

When Alexander the Great, the great world conqueror, was at the height of his power, he decided to have his portrait painted. The finest artist was called to produce the masterpiece. Arriving at the court, the artist was told that Alexander the Great wanted a full-face pose rather than a profile. This bothered the artist because one side of Alexander's face was disfigured by a long scar. After studying the subject for some time, the painter thought of a way to cover the blemish. He seated Alexander the Great at a table. Then, placing the general's elbow on the table, he asked him to cup his chin in his hand. And as a final thoughtful touch, the artist skillfully arranged the fingers in such a way that they completely hid the scar. At last, fully satisfied with the effect, he went to work with his paint and brushes and produced a historic portrait of his famous subject.

That is what agape love does — it minimizes the shortcomings and mistakes of others.

• Agape love is truthful and optimistic. It "does not rejoice in unrighteousness, but rejoices in the truth . . . believes all things, hopes all things, endures all things." When Paul talks in verse 7 about believing all things, he is not recommending gullibility. In verse 6 he indicates that agape love rejoices in that which is true. It doesn't rejoice in gossip. It doesn't rejoice in innuendo or deception. Agape love rejoices in truth and practices righteousness or right living.

Paul means then that we give the other person the benefit of the doubt. The *Amplified Bible* translates the verse in this way. "Love is ever ready to believe the best of every person." Many times one partner in a marriage will shout, "I can't trust him until he earns my trust." That kind of attitude will further erode a marriage, because we will be always suspicious of the other person. But agape love demands that as parents, spouses, church members, we not be overly suspicious of others' methods and motives, but prefer, if anything, to give too much trust as opposed to too little.

If there is one thing that is a breeding ground for destruction in a home or a church or a relationship, it is suspicion. Destructive conflict breeds rapidly when we refuse to trust one another. There is no hope for a relationship to grow, as long as one person holds suspicion over the other. Mistrust is a killer of companionship and the conflict which arises out of it destroys with a vengeance. That is why Paul says that agape love believes all things—it is not suspicious.

Dr. Lewis Smedes in his book, *Caring and Commitment,* has an extended but helpful word for us. He is speaking here of the marriage relationship:

> When I commit myself to you I expect you to trust me. You know that I'm capable of leaving you. You know that I can let you down. So I make my commitment and expect you to trust me to keep it.
>
> But then I need to trust you too. I have to trust you not to abuse my commitment, not to scorn it, not to deflate it. I trust that you will not turn me away when I want to be present with you. I trust that you will treat my commitment kindly.
>
> Trust is our only guarantee. But this is not a guarantee

at all, not in the sense of a sure thing backed by a contract that can hold up in court. We can draw up a contract between us, and my contract may limit your losses
if I should leave you, or mine if you should leave me. But
no contract can tell us for sure that I will stay with you
or you with me when staying costs us something.

Our trust is not blind. Our inner eye, our heart, has its
own way of seeing. We trust because our inner eye sees
each other's sincerity and character. And what we see
reduces the risk. It does not insure against pain, not the
way Lloyds of London can insure against disaster. But it
offers us the peculiar kind of hope that dares to take the
high risk of personal commitment. Without trust, nobody
in his or her right mind would ever make a serious commitment to another individual. With trust, a person dares
to gamble on a lasting partnership of caring love.[9]

Be aware that agape love also hopes all things. That is, it
hopes for better things. Love is optimistic. I have been
described as an eternal optimist. But there are days when
I wonder if my optimism is worth holding on to. Let me
explain. We all blow it more than we'd like. Just chart your
history for one day and you'll know that that's true. But
we also do some things correctly. Agape love takes the
positive truths about others, about the family and the
church that we belong to, and rejoices in those aspects of
that person or that organization and then trusts that God
will work on the other areas that perhaps aren't so positive.
Our problem is that we like to play God with other people's
lives. We have a tendency to see the problems, not the
positives.

Now I have a challenge test for you. On the chart, under
Home and *Church* write five things that you are thankful
for, that are a cause of rejoicing, that are positives. That
may keep you busy for a long time, if you are not given to
noting positives.

Now, here's the test. For the next three days, whenever
the subjects of church and home come into your conversa-

REASONS TO BE THANKFUL
Home
1.
2.
3.
4.
5.
Church
1.
2.
3.
4.
5.

tion, talk only about those five items of rejoicing that you have listed. No complaining, no whining. For some people, this may seem an impossible assignment, because they have never gone three days running without complaining about something in one of those two categories. This is an assignment, however, that agape love would accept.

• Agape love is permanent. "Love never fails. . . . But now abide faith, hope, love, these three; but the greatest of these is love" (vv. 8, 13). In verse 8 Paul is using the strongest language of negation. In fact, he's piling up words to get his point across because the word *never* is actually a combination of three Greek words in a row that literally mean, "not even at any time will love fail." Paul's thrust is that love never falls away, never disappears; it never quits or is used up. Love keeps on coming. The more you use it, the more there is. When you begin to exercise agape love, you find yourself able to exercise it all the more. And the more that you give it away, the more you seem to have to give away.

Everything in this life is temporary, lacking in some measure, with the exception of agape love. It never fades, it will never collapse, it will never terminate. If we want to spend our time on what is eternal and will not change when eternity dawns, agape love is what we want.

When Dr. Joseph Parker preached in the City Temple of London, he spoke of the character of Christians.

> They will never believe evil of one another; they will never take any outside reports about one another; they will dwell within themselves, they will live the life of brotherhood. . . .
>
> Knit together in love. Who can estimate the strength of that binding force? What has love not done? If we love one another, we should look for the virtues rather than the vices, the excellencies rather than the defects. . . . There is plenty of criticism in the world, (selfish,) hostile, bitter, clamorous criticism. There is nothing so easy to find as fault. . . . Dreadful is the life that is unblessed with love — a cold, mean, poor life; its bread is unsanctified, its very prosperity is but the higher aspect of failure, and all its ambition is an irreligious prayer addressed to an irreligious god.
>
> Rich is the life that is full of love. . . . And herein is the strength of the church. Love will sustain every burden, see a way through every difficulty, have a happy answer to every enigma, and will hold out a hopeful hand to every case of necessity.
>
> If we say that we are knit together in love, we are saying that we are knit for time, for eternity, for earth, for heaven. For love is the universal language, and like its Author, love will never die.[10]

Some time ago I came across a book for children, *The Velveteen Rabbit,* that contains a message for adults. The main character in the book is a little stuffed rabbit, all shiny and new, who goes through the process of becoming "real," that is, more than just a toy on a shelf. As he struggles with those initial feelings of uneasiness, he engages an old, worn-out, well-used, much loved stuffed horse in conversation.

The Skin Horse had lived longer in the nursery than any of the other animals. He was so old that his brown coat was bald in patches and showed the seams underneath, and most of the hairs in his tail had been pulled out to string bead necklaces. But he was wise, for he had seen a long succession of mechanical toys arrive to boast and swagger and, by and by, break their mainsprings and pass away, and he knew that they were only toys, and would never turn into anything else. For nursery magic is very strange and wonderful, and only those playthings that are old and wise and experienced like the Skin Horse understand all about it.

"What is REAL?" asked the Rabbit one day, when they were lying side by side near the nursery fender, before Nana came to tidy the room. "Does it mean having things that buzz inside you and a stick-out handle?"

"Real isn't how you are made," said the Skin Horse. "It's a thing that happens to you. When a child loves you for a long, long time, not just to play with, but REALLY loves you, then you become real."

"Does it hurt?" asked the Rabbit.

"Sometimes," said the Skin Horse, for he was always truthful. "When you are Real you don't mind being hurt."

"Does it happen all at once, like being wound up," the Rabbit asked, "or bit by bit?"

"It doesn't happen all at once," said the Skin Horse. "You become. It takes a long time. That's why it doesn't often happen to toys who break easily, or have sharp edges, or who have to be carefully kept. Generally, by the time you are Real, most of your hair has been loved off, and your eyes drop out and you get loose in the joints and very shabby. But these things don't matter at all, because once you are real you can't be ugly, except to people who don't understand."[11]

2
THE HEART OF LOVE

*Let love be without hypocrisy. Abhor what is evil;
cling to what is good. Be devoted to one another
in brotherly love; give preference to one another
in honor; not lagging behind in diligence,
fervent in spirit, serving the Lord;*

*rejoicing in hope, persevering in tribulation,
devoted to prayer, contributing to the needs
of the saints, practicing hospitality.*

Romans 12:9-13

I t was a best-seller for several months. Coming out of nowhere as it did, I wondered if it was the title that initially vaulted the book into public view. But as I read and then reread Robert Fulghum's *All I Really Need to Know I Learned in Kindergarten,* it became obvious to me that it wasn't just the title.

In the early dry dark of an October's Saturday evening, the neighborhood children are playing hide-and-seek. How long since I played hide-and-seek? Thirty years; maybe more. I remember how. I could become part of the game in a moment, if invited. Adults don't play hide-and-seek. Not for fun, anyway. Too bad.

Did you have a kid in your neighborhood who always hid so good nobody could find him? We did. After awhile we would give up on him and go off, leaving him to rot wherever he was. Sooner or later he would show up, all mad because we didn't keep looking for him. And we would get mad back, because he wasn't playing the game the way it was supposed to be played. There's HIDING and there's FINDING, we'd say. And he'd say it was hide-and-seek, not hide-and-give-up, and we'd all yell about who made the rules and who cared about who, anyway, and how we wouldn't play with him anymore if he didn't get it straight, and who needed him anyhow and things like that. Hide-and-seek-and-yell. No matter what, though, the next time he would hide too good again. He's probably still hidden somewhere for all I know.

As I write this, the neighborhood game goes on, and there is a kid under a pile of leaves in the yard just under my window. He has been there a long time, now, and everybody else is found and they are about to give up on him over at the base. I considered going out to the base and telling them where he is hiding. And I thought about setting the leaves on fire to drive him out. Finally, I just yelled, "GET FOUND, KID," out the window. And scared him so bad he probably . . . started crying and ran home to tell his mother. It's real hard to know how to be helpful sometimes.

A man I know found out last year he had terminal cancer. He was a doctor. And knew about dying . . . so he kept his secret. And died. Everybody said how brave he was . . . but privately his family and friends said how angry they were that he didn't need them, didn't trust their strength. . . . He hid too well. Getting found would have kept him in the game. Hide-and-seek, grown-up style. Wanting to hide. Needing to be sought. Better than hide-and-seek, I like the game called Sardines. In Sardines the person who is It goes and hides, and everybody goes looking for him. When you find him, you get in with him and hide there with him. Pretty soon everybody is hiding together, all stacked in a small space like puppies in a pile. And pretty soon somebody giggles and somebody laughs and everybody gets found.

"Olly-olly-oxen-free." The kids out on the street are hollering the cry that says, "Come on in, wherever you are. It's a new game." And so say I to all those who have hid too good, "GET FOUND, KID! Olly-olly-oxen-free."[1]

At one time or another, you have hidden under stacks of leaves. You carefully arranged them so that they would cover every part of you, and for a while it was exciting to watch those who were searching for you walk right by and not see you. But it is no longer any fun. The leaves are dry and dead. They scratch your face, and some of them have rotted and smell. Now you want to be found, but you've hidden too well.

Or maybe your experience with the leaves was different. You were supposed to be the finder, not the hider. But you were not interested in the game . . . you were too wrapped up in yourself to spend time seeking others. And although you knew where some were hiding . . . you never walked their way.

THE SINCERITY OF LOVE

Like a giant lawn rake, Romans 12 sweeps away the leaves and asks us either to allow ourselves to be found . . . or at least to keep looking for others. Notice how the game begins in verse 9, "Let love be without hypocrisy."

This word for love is *agape*, a word taken over by the first Christians as they sought to find language to express their experience of God's grace. It was filled with new meaning and significance by the earliest Christians as they reveled in God's love for them. And it is crucial for our understanding to realize that a love which sweeps away the leaves, which reaches out to other people, is riveted to God's love for us. Our love for others is sourced in God's love for us.

But more than that, agape love has to do with the mind. It is not simply an emotion, but is a principle by which we deliberately live. It's a directional guide in our lives. But that direction is not something we toy with. It's not something casually manufactured at select moments. Directional love must have a depth of sincerity to it. That's why it must be "without hypocrisy." Those words mean "without play-acting or pretending." The hypocrite of the first century was the actor who projected an image but hid his true identity behind a mask. In order for our love to reflect the love of God, it must be sincere; it must be genuine. The moment it is faked, it withers and fades.

I think that there is a temptation for believers to claim virtues that we in fact do not possess. This can make us feel better about ourselves, even as we hide under the leaves. But the writers of the New Testament consistently look for sincerity, especially when it is a question of love. The Latin word for *sincere* means "without wax." You see, the ancients had developed a very expensive porcelain which was greatly valued. Often when it was fired in the oven, tiny cracks would appear, ruining the product. Dishonest merchants would smear pearly-white wax over these cracks to pass it off as flawless porcelain. And it worked, unless the buyer was sharp enough to hold that porcelain vase up to the light of the sun, for then he could see the flaws. Honest dealers marked their flawless works with the words, *sine cera* — without wax.[2] Paul tells us that this is how our love should be.

This does not mean that in the name of love we are to surrender our ability to be discerning. The second phrase of verse 9 says, "Abhor what is evil; cling to what is good." The word *evil* means "that which is morally evil, specifically, that which directly injures others." A love that says yes to everything and everyone is hypocritical; it is playacting. True love makes moral choices. It doesn't flounder in a sea of relativity. You see, love is very different from sentimentality. True love involves a deep hatred for all that is evil, because evil can never benefit the person loved.

When true biblical love faces evil, it will stand against it. It won't pretend that there is no evil, or that the evil is right, for that would smack of hypocrisy. On the other hand, when good is evident, love comes to its rescue and clings to it. It is popular today to love everything, regardless if it is good or bad. It's like the bumper sticker that reads: "Honk, if you believe in anything." Our text shouts that the person who really loves, with the deep fervor of agape love, will have a holy hatred for every evil thing, but will cling to what is good.

The difficulty for us is that if we keep hiding under the leaves, behind the masks, we will never get close enough to be able to cling to relationships and people who are good. We'll be hiding instead. In an attempt to hide from the evil in life, we can also hide from the good. That is not a balanced approach. While we certainly must not surrender our moral values, we need to concentrate on clinging actively to that which is good. But to do this, we have to crawl out from under the leaves. We have to be willing to be found by others. We won't continue to build protective walls; we won't crawl into a corner and try to make it alone. We need good people to cling to.

Relating to people is what love is all about. One person defines love this way: "Love is an ACTIVITY, not a passive effect; it is a 'standing in,' not a 'falling for.' In the most general way, the active character of love can be described by stating that love is primarily giving, not receiving."[3]

Paul would have concurred with that. In the remaining verses he tells us how love acts toward others.

THE DEVOTION OF LOVE

"Be devoted to one another in brotherly love" (v. 10). The word for *brotherly love* describes the natural affection of parents and children, brothers and sisters. Paul is reminding us that Christians are to see themselves as a family. God is our spiritual Father and we are brothers and sisters spiritually; as members of the body of Christ, we should be doing everything in our power to remain devoted to each other. Now certainly, family love doesn't mean that there will never be any problems or disagreements. It does, however, mean the kind of devotion which recognizes and can speak about weaknesses and failures, but with a quality of loyalty that outlasts disappointments. That is what families are all about . . . consistent, long-term love, the kind of love expressed by an anonymous young author:

When you thought I wasn't looking, I saw you hang my first painting on the refrigerator, and I wanted to paint another one. When you thought I wasn't looking, I saw you feed a stray cat, and I thought it was good to be kind to animals. When you thought I wasn't looking, I saw you make my favorite cake just for me, and I knew that little things are special things. When you thought I wasn't looking, I heard you say a prayer, and I believed there is a God I could always talk to. When you thought I wasn't looking, I felt you kiss me good-night, and I felt loved. When you thought I wasn't looking, I saw tears come from your eyes, and I learned that sometimes things hurt, but, it's all right to cry. When you thought I wasn't looking, I saw that you cared, and I wanted to be everything that I could be. When you thought I wasn't looking, I looked . . . and wanted to say thanks for all the things I saw when you thought I wasn't looking.

That's family love. But this devotion easily becomes muddled because we're so preoccupied with our own agendas, our own formulas, our own pursuits. That's why Paul wrote, "Give preference to one another in honor" (v. 10).

Self-pursuit grates against love like fingernails scraping across a chalkboard. The result of true love is that we do not seek our own honor or position, but are willing to give honor and respect to others. Paul is asking us to outdo each other in giving honor, and giving honor simply means "to give recognition, to show appreciation, and to demonstrate respect."

This honoring is not based on personal attractiveness or usefulness, but rather on the fact that you as a Christian have Christ in your heart. Paul is telling you not to push for first place. This doesn't mean you pretend to appreciate someone, or offer false praise, or act as if you are a zero yourself. That's back to hypocrisy. What Paul is pushing for is true humility and love which eagerly seeks for and rejoices in and honors the good qualities in other believers.

When you're around people you're supposed to love, what do you look for? Do you watch for their mistakes, their foul-ups so that you can pounce? Do you examine their lifestyles for areas of weakness so that you can then criticize? Do you watch them performing a task and then rehearse how you could have done it better? If you do, don't be surprised if the people you're supposed to love are hiding so well that you can't find them.

I like J.B. Phillips' paraphrase of this verse: "Be willing to let other men have the credit." If you really don't care who gets the credit, you can enjoy yourself and also excel at love. And yet how rare that is. William Barclay, whose New Testament word studies stand apart from the rest, cuts to the heart of it when he writes: "More than half the trouble that arises in the church concerns rights and privileges and places and prestige. Someone has not been given his or her place; someone has been neglected or unthanked; someone has been given a more prominent place on a platform than someone else and there is trouble."[4]

The date was December 10, 1986; the place was Jacksonville, Florida. Richard Rominez, a teenager, was terminally ill with muscular dystrophy, and a local charity had arranged for him to go on a free shopping spree. All the clerks and managers of the store watched as this dying teenager was allowed to take anything he wanted. Everything he reached for was for someone else . . . gifts for his father, his mother, his two brothers, and *nothing* for himself.

This so astounded the managers of the store that they wouldn't allow the charity to pay for the shopping spree. They spoke of it as "making" their Christmas.

By the following April, Richard was dead. But ever since, carefully selected teenagers are allowed to go on free shopping sprees in Jacksonville, all because of the unselfish spirit of Richard Rominez.[5]

THE DILIGENCE OF LOVE

Romans 12:11 says, "Not lagging behind in diligence, fervent in spirit, serving the Lord." When a person comes into a personal relationship with Jesus Christ through faith, he gains a greater understanding and appreciation of God's love. And out of that appreciation for God's love there grows a desire to express that love to others through service. But this expression of love is not to be of a casual, yawning kind. The thrust of this verse is that the Lord's service calls for our best. Love exercised in service for Christ has a burning intensity to it that is costly.

This verse is an all-out attack on casual Christianity and on anything that hints of laziness or halfheartedness. It pictures enthusiastic, white-hot believers *acting lovingly* out of conviction and commitment to Christ. In fact, the verb translated as *fervent* literally means "boiling over in spirit." There is to be an effervescence to our life, to our love, to our service. One commentator explains it this way: "Believers should earnestly ask the Holy Spirit to fill them with zeal, the enthusiasm needed for properly carrying out their Christian duties and attaining their goal. Then they will not be passive, but with joy and enthusiasm will address themselves to the task of actually and wholeheartedly serving the Lord."[6]

There is something exciting about enthusiasm. The word itself comes from two Greek words, *en* and *theos. En* means "in," and *theos* means "God." An enthusiastic Christian then is "in God" or "full of God." I am so tired of boring, routine Christians who can't spell enthusiasm, let alone model it. And yet one of the things that keeps love alive is enthusiasm and excitement. A.W. Tozer was so correct when he wrote:

> Among the churches one scarcely finds a believer whose blood count is normal and whose temperature is up to standard. The flush and excitement of the soul in love must be sought in the New Testament or in the biographies of the saints; we look for them in vain among the professed followers of Christ in our day. The low level of moral enthusiasm among us may have a significance far deeper than we are willing to believe.[7]

What is your level of enthusiasm when it comes to serving Christ through love? Some of us are so boring, so predictable, so unenthused about life, about Christ, about love. Everything we do is a chore, a grind, a bother. We bring shadows to sunshine, we're like sticky doorknobs in a spotless room. We've lost our appreciation for Christ's love and our enthusiasm for life and service.

Do you remember Billy Sunday? People marveled that this man with about a fourth-grade education would get so excited when he talked about either Christ or Satan that he would tear off part of his clothing. Yet men of intellect and culture would hang on his every word. Why? Because he had a conviction of sincerity that they couldn't quite understand.

You would have to go a long way back to understand it. You would have to go back to his mother's pregnancy, because Billy Sunday was born four months after his father was killed in the Civil War.

When Billy was six and his older brother eight, their mother took them to a hotel where they spent the night. At 4 A.M. she wakened them. Then with tears streaming down her face, she kissed each of them.

"Never forget that I love you," she said, "but I can't afford to raise you. I'm sending you to the Veterans Orphans Home in Glenwood, Iowa."

Then she put the two little boys on the train with two tickets. En route they got hungry. They got off at one stop, wandered into a hotel and asked for food.

When they were told the prices, they turned their pockets inside out and explained they were hungry. The woman behind the counter broke down crying.

"My husband was killed in the Civil War," she sobbed. "I'll feed you." And she did.

They then got back on the train. When the conductor, who had just gotten on, took their tickets, he said, "These tickets don't go as far as Glenwood. I'll have to put you off."

Billy pleaded and cried, "I got no money 'cause I got no daddy."

The conductor looked at them and assured them, "I fought in the war; nobody will put you off this train."

He took them to the orphans' home; and for the next seven years he was the only person with whom they had outside contact, for he visited them regularly.

You must know that to understand Billy Sunday. He never lost his appreciation for the impact of love. Christ's love in his young life had filled him with enthusiasm.

THE DETERMINATION OF LOVE

When you start to detail love, you are confronted with its devotion, its diligence, and also with its determination. In verse 12 we read, "Rejoicing in hope, persevering in tribulation, devoted to prayer."

In their game of hide-and-seek, some people are so well hidden, so deeply buried with leaves, that even if you find them and dig them out, they resist your love. They fight you off. They make it very difficult to love them. But that is where hope steps in, for hope focuses on the future. It continually looks beyond the present difficulties and refuses to get bogged down in today.

People can be difficult, even when you try to love them. But hope looks for the possibilities and potential in them. When their pants are torn and their knees are bleeding again, hope finds the Band-Aid and applies the patch. When their eyes are on fire and their words are aflame, hope brings the anger under control. When their makeup has run and their face is tear-stained, hope offers a Kleenex and another chance.

This is true even when the people you are trying to love have lives filled with pain and bring their pain to you. In the middle of verse 12, the word *tribulation* means "to squeeze, to compress, to crush." That happens sometimes when you reach out to others. But Paul reminds us that love has the power that is needed to bear up persistently even under that kind of stress, that kind of pain, that kind of suffering.

You see, the Christian life inevitably involves suffering because suffering with others is an activity of love. It is love that bears hurts. It is love that takes the blame, that is willing to endure. Anyone who is called to be a Christian must learn to love during times of pain.

Love for others continues because of hope. Even when people and circumstances seem to run against you, agape love looks for the best. Even facing into the jaws of pain, love keeps on pulling the leaves away. And one of the reasons you can keep on is because you bathe the entire process in prayer. You are "devoted to prayer." There are times when you get tired of always searching to find somebody to love, because inevitably you get hurt in the process. So what can you do? Tell the Lord about it. You see, He knows the risks of love.

Please understand that all the hope, all the perseverance, all the prayer in the world won't take away the risk involved in love. There is always a risk involved. Jay Kesler, President of Taylor University, tells the story about the time he was at a youth camp. He got a call from his wife. She said, "You've got to come home . . . something awful's happened."

Jay's brother-in-law, Ted, drove a milk truck. Partway through his route, he decided to go home. Each day he picked up one of his kids and today it was Tammy, his six-year-old. She got in and he backed out of the driveway. Just then, Tammy changed her mind and hopped out. Ted didn't see her; put the truck in drive, and ran over her.

Tammy got up and ran across the yard crying, "Mommy, help me," and then fell over. They rushed her to a hospital where she died six hours later. Her mother said to Jay, "I wish we never had had Tammy, then it wouldn't hurt so bad."

A half hour later she said, "But that's the way it is. If you love somebody, it will hurt."

THE GENEROSITY OF LOVE

There is one more detail of love that we must embrace. In our polished churches and well-ordered social circles, this detail tugs at our coattails and begs for attention: "Contributing to the needs of the saints, practicing hospitality" (v. 13).

Christians who are fueled by love will not doubt their obligation to help meet the physical needs of fellow Christians. We're talking here about legitimate, documented needs related to financial and daily necessities. Paul is suggesting that those of us who want to demonstrate the heart of love are to so identify ourselves with the needs of other Christians that we make them our own.

Someone has said, "Love is . . . the commitment of my will to your needs and best interests, regardless of the cost to me." Does that make sense to you? Even if it does, is it something you do?

For every person who cries out to you for help, there may be a thousand others who are entitled to your attention. But that is a poor excuse for not helping the person whose cries you hear. Yet, how do you determine who to help? You reach out and take hold of the one who happens to be nearest.

Love meets needs and it opens its home along with its heart. Christians traveled widely in the first century and it was important that wherever they went they could find hospitality among believers. They were all one family and they were readily welcomed as guests even by believers they had never met.

Do you realize that if 100 families in a church opened their homes one night a week to a stranger, in a year they would have ministered to over 5,000 people? There would be no expense to the church and no involvement in a new program. But they would reach their community, and keep people from being hidden by the leaves. Bruce Larson said it best:

The neighborhood bar is possibly the best counterfeit there is to the fellowship Christ wants to give His Church. It's an imitation, dispensing liquor instead of grace, escape rather than reality, but it is a permissive, accepting and inclusive fellowship. It is unshockable. It is democratic. You can tell people secrets and they usually don't tell others or even want to. The bar flourishes not because most people are alcoholics, but because God has put into the human heart the desire to know and be known, to love and be loved, and so many seek a counterfeit at the price of a few beers. Christ wants His Church to be unshockable, democratic, permissive — a fellowship where people can come in and say, "I'm sunk! I'm beat! I've had it!" Alcoholics Anonymous has this quality. Our churches too often miss it.[8]

> I'm a child playing hide-and-seek
>   waiting for someone to find me
>   and you call my name
>   and say, "You're it!"
>   And You did it, Lord!
>   You found me hiding
>   in the silliest, saddest places,
>   behind old grudges . . .
>   under tons of disappointments . . .
>   tangled up in guilt,
>   smothered with success,
>   choking on sobs that nobody hears.
> You found me
>   and You whispered my name
>   and said, "You're it!"
> And I believe You mean it . . .
> And now maybe
>   the silent tears can fall out of my throat . . .
>   get wet on my cheeks . . .
> And now maybe
>   I don't have to play hide-and-seek anymore.
> "OLLY, OLLY, OXEN FREE,"
> Come on in, wherever you are, it's a new game.
>   Author Unknown

I think of a Presbyterian elder in Pittsburgh, Pennsylvania, who got a call one night. It was not an ordinary night—it had rained and then everything had frozen. The whole city was covered with ice. Police wagons and fire wagons were not moving. Ambulances from hospitals were not on the road.

This elder got a call from the pastor of his church. There was a family in the church whose young son had leukemia. The youngster had suddenly taken a turn for the worse. The parents called the hospital and were told to bring him in, since the hospital was unwilling to send an ambulance. Because the parents didn't have a car, they called the minister of their church asking if he would help. His car was in the repair shop some ten miles from his home. But the elder happened to live near the family, and so the minister called him.

The elder had three accidents before he got to the home of the family. He couldn't stop for stop signs or traffic lights. He could stop only when the momentum of his car was stopped by an object.

The parents brought the little boy down wrapped in a blanket. The mother and the child got into the front seat, the father in the back seat, and they started off. They had several minor scrapes as they went along the road. As they came to the bottom of a hill and managed to skid to a stop, the elder had to decide whether he should try to make the grade on the left or whether he should go to the right and down the valley to the hospital. And as he was thinking about this, he chanced to look to the right and saw the little boy. The youngster's face was flushed, and his eyes wide with fever and with fear. To comfort the child, he reached over and tousled his hair. Then it was that the little boy said to him, "Mister, are you Jesus?"

Do you know, in that moment he could almost have said, "Yes," for him to live was Jesus Christ.[9]

3
WHEN LOVE
SHORT-CIRCUITS

This you know, my beloved brethren.
But let every one be quick to hear, slow to speak
and slow to anger; for the anger of man
does not achieve the righteousness of God.

Therefore putting aside all filthiness
and all that remains of wickedness, in humility
receive the word implanted, which is able
to save your souls.

James 1:19-21

A number of years ago, *Psychology Today* reported the results of a poll of more than 650 readers. The typical reader of that magazine is forty-five years old or younger, and has had at least two years of college. The question they posed was: "If you could secretly push a button and thereby eliminate any person, without any repercussions to yourself, would you press that button?"

Sixty percent said, "Yes, I would press the button!" When asked if they had anyone specific in mind, men generally chose public figures. Women tended to select bosses, ex-husbands, or men who had victimized them sexually.

Significantly, many people extended the button's power to include entire groups. Violent criminals, rapists, and murderers were targeted for execution because, as one thirty-eight-year-old woman put it: "You should have the freedom to feel safe."

But one twenty-nine-year-old man posed an intriguing question to the magazine that suggests the pervasiveness of anger in our society: "If such a device were invented, *would anyone live to tell about it?*"[1]

I wonder how many of us would escape the button. I wonder how many of us wish we had a mailing address so that we could place our order. Many of us no longer lead

lives of quiet desperation. We are for the most part in a
state of contained anger. And yet we should not be surprised. Anger, as a way of life, is nothing new. One observ-
er writes:

> Americans, very many of them, are obsessed with ten-
> sions. Nerves are drawn tense and twanging. Emotions
> boil up and spill over into violence largely in meaning-
> less or unnatural directions. In the cities people scream
> with rage at one another, taking out their unease on the
> first observable target. The huge reservoir of the anger of
> frustration is full to bursting. The cab driver, the bus or
> truck driver, pressed with traffic and confusion, de-
> nounces (everyone and everything). A line has formed for
> the couches of the psychoanalysts of people wound so
> tight that the mainspring has snapped and they deliver
> their poisons in symbolic capsules to the doctor. . . . Of
> love, only the word, bent and (defiled), remains."[2]

John Steinbeck wrote those words in 1966. Yet he could
have written them today or 2,500 years ago. The verdict
would be the same, because anger, like a slow-growing
cancer, like termites working silently but efficiently beneath the surface, is seemingly always with us but not often
enough detected or exterminated until it's too late.

The first century, like our own, was a time of unrest, its
voracious appetite fed and fueled by the explosive emotions
of its citizens. There was constant conflict—politically and
religiously. But behind all of that, often denied or rational-
ized, was the intense conflict of relationships. And that
conflict was not reserved for the inner-city ghettos any
more than for penthouse apartments. It was a conflict that
marched arrogantly and confidently down the aisles of the
churches, prompting, pushing, forcing Paul, the great
missiologist and sociologist of his era, to write, "Love is
patient" (1 Corinthians 13:4).

It is no accident that as Paul thought his way through the
subject of love, he began with a behavior that short-circuits
love. He begins by exposing the raw edges of our hostility.

You see, the word *patient* comes from the Greek word *makrothumos*. *Makro* means "a long way from"; *thumos* means "anger." The suggestion is that those of us who demonstrate love for others take a long time before igniting and bursting into flames. As it is used in the New Testament, the word *patience* refers to our composure, our even temper with people, not with our circumstances. It is prolonged restraint from anger. But more than that, patience with people is not so much a character trait but *a way of life* that grows out of love. In fact, it is the primary expression of love.

Now even people who love each other at times get unreasonable, angry, hurt, sulky, frustrating, inappropriate, and downright foolish. These are not necessarily evidences of lack of love, for when people love, these bumps in the road pass faster if they are loyal, helpful, and supportive of each other even in those difficult moments. But constant anger and hostility erode and will ultimately destroy relationships of love.

THE ANGER OF MAN

When Paul talked about patience, he used the word *thumos,* which describes turbulent, passionate outbursts of temper. But there is another word for anger in the New Testament that James, the half brother of Jesus, knew about. It's a word that describes not temper, but something deeper, more insidious—a chronic, constant, bubbling beneath the surface.

Lurking in the dimly lit shadows of our life, hiding behind the rafters, scurrying for cover at the slightest hint of discovery but feeding the beast of temper, is this chronic species of anger. It's the anger that keeps you awake at night, that gives you heartburn, that clenches your teeth when you ought to be smiling. It's an anger that seems to elude identification—you can't seem to find a cause for it.

But you have discovered one thing—you know you're always seething inside.

> To walk the streets of a typical American city is to see anger everywhere. To live the competitive life in an urban setting is to feel . . . "angry all the time." No one, of course, is angry all the time, any more than we are frightened all the time. But the hyperbole is closing in on reality, and is fast becoming a description of, a metaphor for, the fast track in every city—a (sign) of what is to come in those areas which may still operate with gentler methods at slower paces. In the past forty years we have seen, I believe, a *frightening* diffusion of anxiety and anger spreading outward from our urban centers and slowly poisoning our general landscape.[3]

It doesn't surprise me that James understood that. As James writes to us in the first chapter of the book that bears his name, it is as if he has been watching our every move during the last month. It appears at times that he is looking over our shoulder, sitting in our car, gulping another coffee and apple fritter with us, while we run from one deadline to another, one crisis to another. He seems to understand our world hauntingly well . . . especially when the subject of anger begins to percolate.

But one of our problems is that we tend to deny that we are angry; we pretend that we don't have difficulty dealing with it in our relationships. That's why James says, "This you know, my beloved brethren. But let everyone be quick to hear, slow to speak and slow to anger" (James 1:19).

He identifies his audience with the words "my beloved brethren." He is talking to Christians. And in introducing his subject of anger he says in effect, "Know this." And then he details some of the things they are to know, but perhaps haven't connected to anger.

● The first of these revolves around a willingness to listen to others: "Let everyone be quick to hear." When you love someone, you want to listen to them. Partners in a quality marriage make it a habit to listen to each other.

Marriages that struggle have partners who either do not communicate and therefore have nothing to listen to, or talk so much that there is no opportunity to listen.

Effective listening is based on a sincere interest in the other person's feelings and opinions, and an active effort to understand that person. And that is exactly what James is driving at when he tells us to "be quick to hear." Listening is an art that is difficult to master, because it means that we must take an intense interest in the person who is speaking. Listening is the art of closing the mouth and opening the ears and heart. Listening is LOVING someone else as you do yourself. That is, his/her concerns and problems are important enough to be heard.

So often we stumble badly here. An anonymous writer pierces our nonlistening defenses, as she puts together a thoughtful poem entitled simply, "Listen." Lift your antenna for a moment and LISTEN!

> When I ask you to listen to me and you start giving advice,
>> you have not done what I asked.
> When I ask you to listen to me and you begin to tell me why I shouldn't feel that way,
>> you are trampling on my feelings.
> When I ask you to listen to me and you feel you have to do something to solve my problems,
>> you have failed me, strange as that may seem . . .
> So please, just listen and hear me.
> And if you want to talk, wait a few minutes for your turn and I promise I'll listen to you.[4]

Angry people can't make that promise because they are very poor at listening to others. Remember, in order to be effective listeners, we must be concerned about others. Angry people are not. They are upset with people, but they are not concerned about them. And so they don't listen.

In his wonderful book, *After You've Said I Do*, Dwight Hervey Small connects loving and listening.

As it is the nature of love to communicate, to give itself freely and fully, so it becomes the nature of love primarily to listen. Love is the fullest possible affirmation of another person, an affirmation that will express itself in listening while the loved person is speaking. Love seeks to know in order to understand and respond. This is to say that love cares and caring is its essence. The love that cares listens.[5]

● Now it stands to reason that to listen well, we must speak less. "Let everyone be ... slow to speak." When all the exceptions and excuses have been made, and all the "ifs" and "buts" accommodated, the unvarnished truth is that we talk too much. Now, this verse is not suggesting that we take a vow of silence. Rather, it suggests that we are to speak with more thought and care and try to be wise in our speech. In other words, we are to think twice before we speak. If we would do that, we often would not say anything. At the very least, we would be more likely to demonstrate sense in our speech.

Unfortunately, our careless words often accompany our angry mood. Angry people consistently, you've discovered, speak before thinking. You can come home whistling the "Mr. Rogers" theme song and an angry person will bite your head off at the door. Not because you're whistling ... not because you're home ... but because they are angry inside.

But the issue goes even deeper. James is cautioning us in our speech because constant talkers cannot hear what anyone else has to say. And invariably, such people have to speak about everything and everyone. Do you ever notice that? They simply must give an opinion on every issue, a verdict on every person brought into a conversation. Dr. A.T. Robertson, the eminent New Testament Greek scholar, describes these people:

The less they know, the more they talk. They have ... opinions on every subject from politics to religion. They know how their neighbors should act in the smallest details and criticize everybody and everything. They are happiest when everyone is on (pins and needles) with talk of some sort; and the more gossipy it is, the better they like it.[6]

One of the greatest enemies of love is gossip. It is death to love. Dr. Theodore Rubin, in his latest book, *Real Love,* pulls no punches when he concludes:

> How can openness possibly be sustained with a chronic gossip? It can't. People who suffer from this affliction sometimes do it out of a need to express hidden hostility. . . . Sometimes they do it in order to be viciously vengeful and on occasion they are conscious of the immediate satisfaction they feel. They are seldom conscious of the connection between their destructive gossip and the LACK OF LOVE in their lives.[7]

Incessant talkers and chronic gossips are rarely good listeners. And never are their ears more tightly closed than when they are angry. You see, those who refuse to listen to others and who are always talking—who are experts on everyone and everything—are often angry people. Why is that? Because they see themselves as the experts, as the ones who are ALWAYS right. When others don't agree with that assessment, their anger escalates and invariably they express that anger in their words.

• The reason so many people have trouble with anger is that they want others to confirm and validate them. They look to others to give an agreeing nod or an affirming vote. When they don't get it, they feel thwarted. Anger becomes their way of responding to their hurt. And so it is no surprise then that James includes a third thing that we know about ourselves and our relationships. "Let everyone be . . . slow to anger."

In case we've missed it, James is here drawing a clear connection, a direct line between our speech and our anger. He is warning against thoughtless, unrestrained anger that leads to rash, harmful, and damaging speech.

And so he advises us to slow down in our anger. The word he uses describes not the temporary outbursts of our temper, but something deeper, more insidious. He writes about a deep-seated kind of anger that is more than a passing irritation or displeasure. It is an anger that rampages toward revenge. It is an anger that is wrapped in the tentacles of persistent hostility and resentment. It is an anger that leaps to hurt others.

Behavioral scientists tell us that this quality of anger usually comes as a result of frustration and that most frustration is caused simply by our not getting our own way.

Now if James had written, "Let everyone be slow to hear, quick to respond and explosive in anger," what kind of person would he be describing? *A very defensive person,* you would say, and you would be correct. Anger and defensiveness often link arms. And what makes it worse is that angry people are usually blind to their hostility.

> Anger begins to surface when a certain individual is even slightly irritated. His/her opinion is challenged, and he is bothered as a result. Such feelings of slight irritation can easily escalate into resentment. Resentment takes an irritation and holds on to it. Bitterness is the next step on the ladder. And bitterness is always communicated . . . others are infected by bitterness. (And) bitterness can quickly result in outrage, revenge, and ultimately violence.[8]

There is only one way to gain perspective in times of potential anger—and that is to back down. Think twice, think three times, count to ten, count to a thousand . . . put everything possible in the way before you place yourself in a position where there is a danger of your anger spilling over into forbidden territory. In case you find this too general, let me suggest some further principles to slow your anger:

—record and review your cynical angry thoughts and feelings. Confide in a friend or your spouse and seek their prayerful support.

—Try to develop empathy and understanding for the other

person. Try to put yourself in their shoes.

–Learn to laugh at yourself. Don't take yourself so seriously.

–Daily immerse yourself in the Scripture . . . starting with Proverbs.

–Practice forgiving others instead of grudge-carrying.

–Pretend this is the last day of your life and put your frustration and anger into that context.[9]

Lincoln's secretary of war, Edwin Stanton, had some trouble with a major general who accused him, in abusive terms, of favoritism. Stanton complained to Lincoln, who suggested that he write the officer a sharp letter. Stanton did so, and showed the strongly worded missive to the President, who applauded its powerful language. "What are you going to do with it?" he asked. Surprised at the question, Stanton said, "Send it." Lincoln shook his head. "You don't want to send that letter," he said. "Put it in the stove. That's what I do when I have written a letter while I am angry. It's a good letter and you had a good time writing it and you feel better. Now, burn it and write another."[10]

James would have liked that counsel, because when we put this verse back together, this is what he has said to us: "Let every person be swift in listening, and slow in speaking, for only then will you be able to avert that angry attitude of heart that seeks to inflict pain in the lives of others."

THE RIGHTEOUSNESS OF GOD

That is James' counsel. But he knew for some of us the warning would have no impact. We would still be tempted to deny our struggle with anger, resentment, and bitterness. Some of us would even attempt to justify it.

And so in the event that we flowed into that kind of current, James reminds us of the direction that a persistent, deep-seated anger always takes by showing us what anger *does not produce.* "For the anger of man does not achieve the righteousness of God" (1:20).

"The righteousness of God" refers to the way of life God requires of Christians — in their thoughts and in their actions. A persistently angry attitude is not the atmosphere in which righteousness flourishes. It is James' conviction that protracted human anger does not further spiritual ends, even when it appears in the garb of religious zeal. For protracted rage and sin are never far apart. Anger is often heavily fortified with the sins of self-importance, self-assertion, intolerance, and stubbornness, to mention a few.

Let's be honest. How many arguments have you really won by overpowering your adversary with anger? How many people have you positively influenced by your anger? How many people have you won to Jesus Christ by your anger? No matter how you slice it, the righteousness of God is not accomplished by anger. Our human anger is always protective and defensive. It always attacks with a sharp barb that seeks to pin people to the wall and leave them there — bloody, embarrassed, and paid back.[11]

Now then, in verse 21, James shows us what *anger does produce.* "Therefore, putting aside all filthiness and all that remains of wickedness." The words *filthiness* and *wickedness* refer to malice, to the attitude of mind that desires the injury of others. You know that bitterness and resentment and anger seem to stick with us indefinitely, often throughout our lives.

Resentment is like a bulldog bite that clenches the teeth of memory into the dead past and refuses to let go. As Dan Hamilton wrote: "Suppressed resentment will never die; it will be held in reserve and nurtured like malignant toadstools in the cellar. Resentment suppressed will never lose its power; like a spark in a gasoline tank, a bit of momentary friction will set off a devastating explosion."[12]

And yet because resentment is so prevalent, we tend to ignore it, to tolerate it. But this verse shows us we must not fail to make the connection between an unwillingness to listen to others, a sinful tongue, and uncontrolled anger, for these are considered as moral filth that must be shed from our lives.

THE HUMBLE HEART

The only question that remains is how? What solutions are there? What alternatives exist? We've considered several already, but they are all summarized best at the end of verse 21: "In humility receive the Word implanted, which is able to save your souls."

Angry people are often not blessed with an attitude of humility. In fact, they are frequently very proud. Deep down in their heart of hearts, angry people think they are right and that everyone else is wrong. As a result, they have no desire to learn from anyone. That is why James offers this advice about being "humbly receptive" of God's Word, His truth. That truth will come to you from your own personal study of the Bible, and from the godly counsel of people you trust. But before any of that can be appropriated, your attitude must be correct. That's why the word *humility* is key here, for humility is the attitude which says a simple yes to what the Word of God teaches and commands. It is, according to John Calvin, "the mind disposed to learn" with prompt readiness.

The verb translated as *receive* means "to welcome with open arms." It is a glad-hearted welcome, which underlines the fact that there should be no resistance on your part to the truth that God has for you. William Barclay describes humility in these words:

> It is the truly teachable spirit. The teachable spirit is docile and (pliable), and therefore humble enough to learn. The teachable spirit is without resentment and without anger and is, therefore, able to face the truth, even when it hurts and condemns. The teachable spirit is not blinded by its own overmastering prejudices, but is clear-eyed to the truth.[13]

It is only as we humbly receive God's truth for our lives that we grow in respect to our salvation and move ahead spiritually. James says we will be "saved," that is, made whole, complete, in all respects.

In a society that has its finger on a button of destruction, in a society where the ability to control anger is disappearing so that, "to walk the streets of a typical American city is to see anger everywhere," *if we, the people of God, the people of His church, would practice love, would act upon what we have learned, would be so concerned with our relationships to each other that we would be willing to do whatever it took to maintain positive relationships,* oh, how the world's perspective of the church would change!

In a sermon entitled "Who Cares?" Dr. Fred Craddock shares an incident from his life that emphasizes the change that would occur in society's impression of the church — if we would only reach out to one another in love instead of anger.

> I grew up hearing criticism of the church. My mother took us to church and Sunday School. My father didn't go. He complained about Sunday dinner being late when she came home. Sometimes the preacher would call and my father would say, "I know what the church wants. The church doesn't care about me. The church wants another name, another pledge, another name, another pledge. Right!" That's what he always said. Sometimes we'd have a revival. Pastor would bring the evangelist and say to the evangelist, "There's one now. Sic him! Get him! Get him!" My father would say the same. Every time my mother was in the kitchen my father said, "The church doesn't care about me. The church wants another name, another pledge." I guess I heard it 1,000 times.
>
> One time he didn't say it. He was in Veterans Hospital. He was down to seventy-three pounds. They had taken out the throat. They had said it was too late. They had put in a metal tube and X ray had burned him to pieces. I flew in to see him. He couldn't speak, he couldn't eat. I looked around the room — potted plants

and cut flowers on all the windowsills. A stack of cards twenty inches deep beside his bed. And even that tray where you put food, if you can eat, on that was a flower. In all the flowers and beside the bed, every card, every blossom, from persons or groups from the church. He saw me read the cards. He could not speak so he took a Kleenex box and wrote on the side of it a line from Shakespeare, and if he had not written this line, I would not tell you the story. He wrote, "In this harsh world, draw your breath in pain to tell my story." I said, "What is your story, Daddy?" And he wrote, "I was wrong."[14]

4
WHEN LOVE TURNS INSIDE OUT

Who among you is wise and understanding?
Let him show by his good behavior his deeds
in the gentleness of wisdom.
But if you have bitter jealousy
and selfish ambition in your heart,
do not be arrogant and so lie against the truth.
This wisdom is not that which comes down from
above, but is earthly, natural, demonic.
For where jealousy and selfish ambition exist,
there is disorder and every evil thing.

James 3:13-16

Jealousy and ambition are twin sisters who refuse to be silenced. Like frenzied, rabid dogs, they nip at our heels and howl at our failures. They feed voraciously on our inadequacies and weaknesses, but are inwardly consumed by the poison of their comparisons and desires. All of us are prey to them. Some of us even enjoy having them around. However, they yield a deadly harvest.

In 1905, Evelyn Nesbit, an American model and showgirl, married millionaire Harry K. Thaw. The following year the couple was dining in a fashionable restaurant when Harry Thaw noticed his wife's former lover, architect Stanford White, at a nearby table. Thaw got up from his table, walked over to White's table, pulled out a gun, and shot his rival three times in the face. He was convicted and judged to be insane.[1] *Insanely jealous!*

Leo Buscaglia accurately exposes the scope and influence of jealousy in our lives when he writes:

> A dictionary definition can, in no way, begin to describe that desperate cluster of feelings we have characterized as jealousy. Powerful and universal as they are, few of us are prepared or equipped to handle them when they suddenly — often without warning — overtake us. This emotion has the power to overwhelm and destroy the

most seemingly sound and secure relationship, the most rational person. At some time or another most all of us have known jealousy. It is no respecter of social position, intellectual or economic level or age.[2]

Ambition, the flip side of jealousy, is just as prevalent. A number of years ago an advertisement appeared in *Fortune* magazine, featuring a diapered baby who was looking you straight in the eye with childlike directness. The line at the top of the picture said: *"We are all created equal. After that, baby, you're on your own."* Then beneath the picture the copy read:

> Nobody's going to hand you success on a silver platter. If you want to make it, you'll have to make it on your own—your own drive, your own guts, your own ambition. Yes, ambition. You don't have to hide it anymore. Society's decided that now it's OK to be up-front about the drive for success. Isn't that what the fast track is all about? If you're one of the fast-track people, your business reading starts with *Fortune.*[3]

Twin sisters—jealousy and ambition, and both killers of love. The love that we are to extend to others has somehow become inverted. It has turned inside out, leaving traces of damage everywhere.

THE GENTLENESS OF WISDOM

In the crowd that James wrote to, there were people who pretty well figured themselves to be on top of things in terms of their careers, and even in the arena of the church. Yet, in their jet-propelled drive to the top, they had been fueled by jealousy and ambition. To these people James wrote: "Who among you is wise and understanding? Let him show by his good behavior his deeds in the gentleness of wisdom" (James 3:13).

On the surface, this verse seems harmless enough. A

wise person who lives closely to God sees more clearly into things than others do, and seems to know how to manage the complexities of life. A person of wisdom is godly in character, sharp in discernment, and helpful in advice and counsel, and is the kind of person you want to have around, especially in the church.

But here's the problem that slowly crawls out of the cocoon of wisdom. Certain people, whose addresses and names James knew, began to put the wisdom of God in their résumés and eventually came to the conclusion that they were hot commodities. But they didn't leave it even at that, for they then began to divide people and churches into categories. These people considered themselves to be "in the know," the ones you would go to when you needed information or counsel. In fact, you might have heard them say, "I don't know why it is, but people just seem to come to me when they have questions or problems about the church." Now, there is nothing necessarily wrong with that—except when the person is controlled by jealousy and ambition.

Some of the people James had in mind just liked to talk big. But others were in fact *jealous* of those who really did have wisdom. They pushed to impress people and to *looooook* good. And that kind of inside-out behavior poisons love. In his book *Real Love,* Theodore Isaac Rubin observes:

> Pride presents us as images of who we want to be rather than our real selves. Proud selves, unfortunately, lack humility, compassion, sensitivity, and the humanity necessary for love. Energy and vitality are used to keep us puffed up and feeling important and sustaining lies about our phony exalted status. Very proud people are extremely difficult to deal with—"Like walking on glass all the time," and (they) make it very difficult to sustain LOVE relationships.
>
> Arrogance makes us truly unlovable. This corrosive makes people attribute qualities to themselves, such as

prestige, power, knowledge, assets, and exalted standing in all areas of life, often beyond human proportion, that they simply don't have. Very arrogant people interpret love as weakness, and as humiliation. They usually decide that superiority is more valuable than love—thus depriving themselves of what they more than anyone need the most.[4]

We sometimes get caught in that trap, don't we? Most of us want to appear "wise," at least in some sphere. When we are not, we feel jealous of others' abilities and influence, and then find ourselves pushing to surpass them.

James challenges us to demonstrate our "wisdom" in the way we live: "Let him show by his good behavior his deeds in the gentleness of wisdom" (v. 13). In other words, if we claim to be wise, then we need to demonstrate our wisdom in our behavior. Wisdom, like love, is a way of life. Someone has defined biblical wisdom as "the ability to apply biblical principles to everyday life. Wisdom is occurring when you glean from the Bible principles for living and then apply them to your life."

Wisdom is not so much revealed by what we say as by *who we are and what we do.* Abraham Heschel, the great Jewish philosopher, once wrote: "To be or not to be is NOT the question. We all want to be. *How to be* and *what not to be* is the essence of the question."

And love, like wisdom, concentrates on who we are and what we do, because it is inherently something we do. Love is an activity directed toward another person. Since it is action, it is a decision—a conscious act of the will. It would be safe to conclude that walking in wisdom includes walking in love.

James reminds us that our wise living is to be marked by gentleness. The word *gentleness* embraces words like "unassuming, unpretentious, and humble." Gentleness is not weakness; it is, in fact, strength under control, strength that is unassuming.

The truly wise person is not feisty, is not a pusher or

grabber, does not attempt to move the spotlight to himself so that others will look his way, consult his point of view first. Instead, the wise person exudes a quiet and humble strength, with nothing to prove. A person who walks in wisdom, who walks in love, is not forcing himself ahead in a jealous, ambitious manner. He is effective, but gentle. Columnist Sydney Harris cuts to the heart of this issue when he observes:

> What the prevailing ethos in modern American life does not seem to understand is that true strength always reveals itself in gentleness and courtesy. Genuine strength of character is always accompanied by a feeling of security that allows one to practice civility and courtesy—but, in our perverse culture, civility and courtesy are often regarded as signs of weakness or some lack of "manliness." And the poor result of our misconception of manhood can be seen in many failing marriages, where the wives uniformly complain that their husbands are just "little boys who failed to grow up."[5]

THE BITTERNESS OF JEALOUSY

While we know that wisdom is demonstrated by folks who have grown up, we so easily keep sliding down the slippery slopes of jealousy and ambition. That's why James reminds us, as well as his contemporaries: "But if you have bitter jealousy and selfish ambition in your heart, do not be arrogant and so lie against the truth. . . . For where jealousy and selfish ambition exist, there is disorder and every evil thing" (vv. 14, 16).

The word *jealousy* actually means "zeal." But the idea behind the word is a fierce desire to promote one's own opinion to the exclusion of the opinions of others. One commentator described jealousy as "a fierce, obstinate, divisive zeal for your own views." It indicates the kind of zeal which does not try to help others, but rather to harm them, since the predominant concern of the jealous person is his own personal advancement.

> Envy is self-corrosive and fatal to relationships, especial-ly with people we envy. Eventually this includes just about everyone. It is an absolute, thorough killer of love. Always wanting what other people have or seem to have makes it impossible to love those people or to receive love from them. Envy tends to be a condition that, once it takes hold, remains malignantly entrenched. When jealousy is chronic we nearly always find envy present, too. Thus the victims of these two (sinister) forces are frightened that something or someone will be taken from them and will always want what someone else seems to have.[6]

But that's not the end of jealousy. James hitched the trailer of bitterness to the jealousy he saw being transported through the churches of his day. Look at verse 14 again: "But if you have bitter jealousy and selfish ambition in your heart . . ." The word *bitter* comes from a verb meaning "to cut." Jealousy egged on by bitterness tries to cut others, to inflict pain, to draw blood—to somehow bring the other person down from a "favored" position. James is addressing this sharpness of spirit in personal relationships, this overconcern for one's own position, dignity, rights.

He is talking about the kind of jealousy "that cannot stand someone else's popularity or success, and given the opportunity, will do anything it can to humiliate and de-grade that person, regardless of who may get hurt in the process."[7] For that is what was going on among the Chris-tians James wrote to. Not only was jealousy lurking menac-ingly in the alleys of their churches, but she was being fostered and nurtured.

An old Greek proverb says, "The envious man dies every time he hears the man he envies (being) praised." How do *you* feel when your best friend is praised for her solo voice? How do you react when your buddy receives acclaim for his academic or athletic ability? How do you relate to those

who are excellent teachers, efficient leaders, popular work-
ers, or capable of making great sums of money? Do you
envy them or thank God for them? Do you complain about
them or encourage them? Do you criticize or compliment
them? When someone else does well, often we'll explain it
away—"He has connections," or, "She got a lucky break."
How do you respond to your husband's success? His whirl-
wind schedule that seems to center stage him while you
wait in the wings? How do you relate to your wife when
she surpasses your level of career accomplishment or spiritual development? Too often we respond with bitter
speech. Max Lucado describes what happens this way:

> Verbal pistols are drawn and a round of words is fired.
> The result? A collision of the hull of your heart against
> the reef of someone's actions. Precious energy escapes,
> coating the surface of your soul with the deadly film of
> resentment. A black blanket of bitterness darkens your
> world, dims your sight, sours your outlook, and suffocates
> your joy. Do you have a hole in your heart?[8]

Bitter envy will drill a hole in your heart and, with
leechlike intensity, will suck the life from you.

● James connects bitter jealousy and selfish ambition.
The words *selfish ambition* refer partly to ambition and
partly to rivalry. They focus both on our tendency to be
self-serving and on our innate inclination to divide and
conquer for personal gain.

In the church, selfish ambition reigns first in a self-serving attitude, the "I want what I want when I want it"
attitude. Selfish ambition is the attitude of self-seekers who
are busy and active in their own interests, who are seeking
their own advantage. Such people are driven, bent on gain-
ing the advantage over others. But this drivenness creates a
monster of incredible appetite because selfish persons are
always anxiously concerned with themselves; they are never satisfied, always restless, driven by the fear of not getting
enough, of missing out, of being deprived. They are filled

with burning envy of anyone who might have more.

These people also long for attention, and if they don't find it, their selfishness takes over and they try to divide a group of people into factions, deliberately attempting to create division. Out of jealousy or resentment, they form exclusive groups which withdraw emotionally or physically from certain other people. They form little pockets off to the side, and if people question them, they respond that "they have the truth, that they are wise, while the rest of the church is wrong."

Sometimes these groups appear in the form of a splinter home Bible study where disagreements are encouraged and then marketed. Sometimes they center on people who come to Sunday School, but boycott the worship services in an attempt to divide. Sometimes they take the shape of church members who won't attend or contribute until a "problem" is taken care of. But in all cases, what such people really want is control . . . they want power. Their love is turned inside out.

THE MOTIVATION TO WISDOM

Now you may be wondering, "Why all the fuss about a little jealousy and selfishness?" The answer lies in the MOTIVA-TION for love turned inside out. "This wisdom is not that which comes down from above, but is earthly, natural, de-monic" (v. 15). If we are controlled by a spirit of jealousy and division, we are proving the presence of a false wisdom that is "earthly." That means that this kind of wisdom eval-uates everything by the standards of society and makes personal gain the highest goal. Earthly wisdom puts ego before everyone and everything else.

But more than that, jealous and selfish behavior find their source in that which is "natural" rather than spiritual. It springs from impulse, rather than thought. This sort of wisdom is also "demonic." Behavior that is consistently

characterized by bitter jealousy and selfish ambition finds
its source not in God but the devil. This false wisdom is not
merely neutral, spurious, or inadequate; it is positively demonic. Whenever we are guilty of having the attitudes and
actions described in these verses, we are being influenced
by demonic forces. But I wonder how many Christians ever
make that connection.

James understood it, as he spoke of the inevitable by-
products of our jealousy and selfish ambition, arrogance and
lying against the truth (v. 14).

Arrogance means "to boast with pride." It carries the
idea of boasting over wrong, of being proud in spite of
being wrong.

Arrogant persons refuse to back down from their position. They refuse to admit they are selfishly ambitious or
bitter or jealous. Their lives and behavior *lie*, as James says,
against the truth of the Gospel and the Word of God, but
they won't admit it. They're in too deep, they've invested
too much, and they don't want to lose face. So they
beligerently maintain a rigid posture of arrogance and
defiance.

They do not recognize that everything they are is contra-
dicted by the truth. When they open their mouths to give
vent to their feelings, they deceive themselves.

When is the last time *you* backed down and admitted you
were wrong? When is the last time *you* acknowledged that
your animosity, your bitterness and divisiveness, at church,
at home, at work, were propelled by jealousy? When is the
last time *you* apologized to anyone for your unwise behavior? You need to, or you will live with the disorder and the
evil that James warns of (v. 16).

Bitter jealousy and ambition always result in disorder.
The term indicates a restless, unsettled state that shows up
first of all in the church. The kind of people described here
constantly plague churches by demanding their own rights
and by exercizing a divisive, party spirit. Instead of bringing people together, they drive them apart. Instead of pro-

ducing harmony, they engender strife. Some of these people possess quick minds and eloquent tongues, but their
impact, nevertheless, on any committee, any board, any
group, is to cause trouble and to disturb and ruin relationships.

The disorder that James refers to impacts yet another
area — the life of jealous and ambitious people themselves.
The tragic truth is that they are never at rest, they are
never content. There is always someone else to envy, some
new mountain to climb, some greater position to attain.
There is an unholy restlessness about people who are consumed with jealousy and selfish ambition. They are de-
stroyed from the INSIDE. Maybe that's you.

After a battle, Alexander the Great was judging various
men for their offenses in battle. One after one, he sen-
tenced them to *death!* Then a very young man came before
his seat of judgment. He was magnificently built, with all
the vitality and the naiveness you find only in the young.

"What is the offense?" Alexander the Great asked.

"Cowardice in battle!" the accused replied.

Everyone hung his head, because *cowardice* was what
Alexander the Great most despised. But suddenly Alexander's face softened and somehow the crowd sensed: "He
too is taken with the man's youth, and with his potential."

"What's your name, sir?" Alexander asked.

"My name is *Alexander*," the young man replied.

With that, Alexander the Great was on his feet: *"Change
your name . . . or change your conduct!"*

There's an old children's chorus that I remember singing.
It has several verses, and the ones I remember most clearly
go like this . . .

"If you're saved and you know it, say Amen."

It has two other really deep verses that say,

"If you're saved and you know it, clap your hands." And

"If you're saved and you know it, stomp your feet."

I had a lot of fun with that song, and you may have too.

But following these action lines are two lines in each verse that are more serious:

IF YOU'RE SAVED AND YOU KNOW IT,
THEN YOUR LIFE WILL SURELY SHOW IT.
Does it?

5
LOVE'S MAGIC EYES

Then Peter came and said to Him,
"Lord, how often shall my brother sin against me
and I forgive him? Up to seven times?"

Jesus said to him, "I do not say to you,
up to seven times, but up to seventy times seven.

"For this reason the kingdom of heaven
may be compared to a certain king
who wished to settle accounts with his slaves.
And when he had begun to settle them,
there was brought to him one who owed him
ten thousand talents. But since he did not have
the means to repay, his lord commanded him
to be sold, along with his wife and children
and all that he had, and repayment to be made.

"The slave therefore falling down,
prostrated himself before him, saying,
'Have patience with me, and I will repay you
everything.'

"And the lord of that slave felt compassion
and released him and forgave him the debt.

"But that slave went out and found one
of his fellow-slaves who owed him
a hundred denarii; and he seized him
and began to choke him, saying,
'Pay back what you owe.'

"So his fellow-slave fell down
and began to entreat him, saying,
'Have patience with me and I will repay you.'

"He was unwilling however, but went
and threw him in prison
until he should pay back what was owed.

"So when his fellow-slaves saw
what had happened, they were deeply grieved
and came and reported to their lord
all that had happened. Then summoning him,
his lord said to him, 'You wicked slave,
I forgave you all that debt
because you entreated me. Should you
not also have had mercy on your fellow-slave,
even as I had mercy on you?'

"And his lord, moved with anger,
handed him over to the torturers
until he should repay all that was owed him.
So shall My heavenly Father also do to you,
if each of you does not forgive his brother,
from your heart."

Matthew 18:21-35

Once upon a time in the village of Faken in innermost Friesland, there lived a thin baker named Fouke. He was a righteous man, with a long thin chin and a long thin nose. Fouke was so upright that he seemed to spray righteousness from his thin lips over everyone who came near him, so much so that the people of Faken preferred to stay away. Fouke's wife, Hilda, was short and round. And her soft roundness seemed to invite people to come close to her in order to share the warm cheer of her heart. Hilda respected her righteous husband, and loved him too, as much as he allowed her. But her heart ached for something more from him than his worthy righteousness.

One morning, having worked since dawn to knead his dough for the ovens, Fouke came home and found a stranger in his bedroom with his wife. Hilda's adultery soon became the talk of the tavern and the scandal of the Faken congregation. Everyone assumed that Fouke would cast Hilda out of his house, so righteous was he. But he surprised everyone by keeping Hilda as his wife . . . saying he forgave her as the Good Book said he should.

In his heart of hearts, however, Fouke could not forgive Hilda for bringing shame to his name. Whenever he thought about her, he felt angry and hard and, in fact, despised her. He only pretended to forgive Hilda so that he could punish her with his righteous mercy. But Fouke's fakery did not sit well in heaven. So each time that Fouke would feel his secret hate toward Hilda, an angel came to him and dropped a small pebble, hardly the size of a shirt button, into Fouke's heart. Each time a pebble dropped, Fouke would feel a stab of pain. Still, he hated Hilda all the more; his hate brought him more pain, and his pain made him hate even more. The pebbles multiplied until Fouke's heart grew heavy with the weight of them, so heavy that the top of his body bent forward so far that he had to strain his neck in order to see straight ahead. Weary with hurt, he began to wish he were dead.

Then one night the angel came to him and told him how he could be healed of his hurt. There was one remedy and only one, for the hurt of a wounded heart. Fouke would need the Miracle of the Magic Eyes. He would need eyes that could look back to the beginning of his hurt and see his Hilda not as a wife who had betrayed him, but as a woman who needed him. Only a new way of looking at things could heal the hurt.

Fouke protested, "Nothing can change the past. Hilda is guilty."

"Yes, poor hurting man, you are right," the angel said. "You cannot change the past, you can only heal the hurt that comes to you from the past. And you can heal it only with the vision of the magic eyes."

"And how can I get your magic eyes?" pouted Fouke.

"Only ask, and they will be given you. Each time you see Hilda through your new eyes, one pebble will be lifted from your aching heart."

Fouke could not ask at once, for he had grown to love his hatred. But the pain of his heart finally drove him to want the magic eyes. And so he asked and the angel gave. And soon Hilda began to change in front of Fouke's eyes as he began to see her as a needy woman who loved him, instead of a wicked woman who had betrayed him.

And the angel kept his promise—he lifted the pebbles from Fouke's heart, one by one. Although it did take a long time to remove them all, Fouke could feel his heart growing lighter. He began to walk straight again, and somehow his nose and chin seemed less thin and less sharp than before. He invited Hilda to come into his heart, and she came, and together they began a journey into a season of humble joy.[1]

SEVENTY TIMES SEVEN

Yes, this is only a fable, but I wish that it were true. I believe that Jesus would like that story. In fact, I am convinced that He would have us see others with magic eyes—with eyes of love, eyes colored with lenses of forgiveness.

When He taught His disciples about forgiveness, it turned out that there was one in the bunch who figured his eyesight was already 20/20 in terms of how he saw people. So a confident and very bold Peter strolled up to Jesus one day and asked, "Lord, if my Christian friend sins against me, I mean, he really fouls me up, gouges me deeply, but I forgive him, what happens when he hurts me again? How many times do I have to put up with that? What I mean, Lord, is, how many times do I forgive him—up to seven times?"

If you're interested in reading his question in your New Testament, you can find it in Matthew 18:21. Now Peter's question is the kind we all ask at some time. We've been pushed, shoved, pounded, and wounded. Each time we have gotten up and started again, but recently we find we aren't getting up quite so quickly, and even after we do we're limping pretty badly. And so we ask this question.

Let's hope we're not making Peter's mistakes in asking. To begin with he was forgetting something. He was sure that the other guy would sin against him, but he didn't mention the possibility of his sinning against someone.

That's pretty true to human behavior. I constantly hear people talk about how much others have hurt them, but they rarely consider how much they have hurt other people. That was Peter.

Also, Peter made the mistake of asking for limits or boundaries to his forgiveness. According to the laws of the Jewish rabbis, the majority opinion was that a person could be forgiven a repeated sin three times, but on the fourth occasion forgiveness didn't apply. Now Peter knew the Lord well enough not to come with that close a boundary. Furthermore, he saw himself as a big-hearted guy, and so, he took the standard of the rabbis, multiplied it by two, and added one for good luck, and figured that Jesus would be impressed with his big heart.

But Jesus wasn't impressed. You see, there was something inherently wrong with Peter's approach. He made it sound as if forgiveness was a commodity that could be weighed and packaged. And then distributed, little by little, up to a certain prescribed point. . . . "Lord, I'm a reasonable person. I'll be more than willing to forgive them. But I want to tell You, when they cross my line, it's all over." Peter was probably thinking about the people he had already forgiven six or seven times. Or about a couple of other disciples who had been driving him crazy for two years, and now he was waiting for Jesus' approval to hammer them. I don't know for sure.

After listening to the offer, Jesus took Peter's breath away with His answer: "I do not say to you, up to seven times, but up to seventy times seven" (v. 22).

You have to know that Peter was sucking wind at this moment. He couldn't believe what he had just heard — Jesus was telling him that a heart of love, a forgiving heart, recognizes no boundaries to forgiveness. The words Jesus used, "seventy times seven," for all practical purposes remove the limits to the extent of forgiveness. And that is incredible when you consider what the word *forgive* itself means. Webster defines it this way: "to cease to feel resentment against an offender or the desire to punish; to pardon; to give up resentment of or claim to requital for an insult; to grant relief from payment of a debt." The essence of the word is the undeserved release of a person from a penalty that could have properly been exacted from or inflicted upon.

There is a wonderful atmosphere of freedom around the word *forgive,* a letting go, a releasing. Forgiveness has the power to soothe, to heal, and to reunite. Our emotional health is dependent to a large degree upon our attitude toward those who offend us. We grow up or wither up depending on our ability to forgive others and to find ways to maintain positive relationships. If we live with an unforgiving heart, we can destroy ourselves emotionally and spiritually.

You may be thinking, "Sure, I can see that for the person who hurts me and then apologizes. But what about the person who doesn't apologize, who shows zero desire to change? What then?"

Well, then you need to be sure the "magic eyes" are really in place and that you forgive that person in your heart. You need to realize that your relationship with them may never go back to where it was — open, honest, caring — until they change. But by forgiving them in your heart, you can go on with your life and not be detoured into the twilight zone of bitterness.

Nobody said this would be easy. But forgiveness is not just words, but is something *you are.* It is not simply a response, "I forgive you," but is the way you live. It does not put off retaliation until a better time, but wipes the slate clean and goes on with life.

Dr. R.V.G. Tasker, Professor Emeritus of New Testament at the University of London, comments on forgiveness:

> The . . . community (of the Messiah) is first and foremost the community of the redeemed. It owes its very existence to the forgiveness made possible by the Messiah's

death. It is the fellowship of men and women for whom Christ died. There is, therefore, laid upon every member the paramount duty . . . of forgiving the personal wrong that may be done to him. Once the willingness to forgive is abandoned, the (reason to be) of the Christian fellowship is lost. The society of the forgiven has no meaning if those who are themselves forgiven, are themselves unforgiving.[2]

Years ago I read a classic story of forgiveness that moves me again as I write it. A woman had kept it locked in her heart for half a century, but shared it with "Dear Abby" to help others in the same position.

> I was twenty and he was twenty-six. We had been married two years and I hadn't dreamed he could be unfaithful. The awful truth was brought home to me when a young widow from a neighboring farm came to tell me she was carrying my husband's child. My world collapsed. I wanted to die. I fought an urge to kill her. And him.
>
> I knew that wasn't the answer. I prayed for strength and guidance. And it came. I knew I had to forgive this man, and I did. I forgave her too. I calmly told my husband what I had learned and the three of us worked out a solution together. (What a frightened little creature she was!) The baby was born in my home. Everyone thought I had given birth and that my neighbor was "helping me." Actually it was the other way around. But the widow was spared humiliation (she had three other children), and the little boy was raised as my own. He never knew the truth.
>
> Was this divine compensation for my own inability to bear a child? I do not know. I have never mentioned this incident to my husband. It has been a closed chapter in our lives for fifty years. But I've read the love and gratitude in his eyes a thousand times.[3]

IT COSTS TO FORGIVE

Peter had never read "Dear Abby," but he did hear another story. Like so many of us, Peter was a visual person, and often Jesus' words didn't make an impression until they came framed in a picture. And so the Lord told Peter a story, recorded for us in Matthew 18:23ff.

A king was at the end of his fiscal year. His debtors came before him, and their debts were called out. One of his employees ended up with a declared debt of 10,000 talents. This could represent $12 million or even up to $1 billion in today's currency. This employee was responsible for collecting taxes. Well he had, but had skimmed a bit off the top in the process. When the auditors finished the books that year, he was in trouble. Despite his pleas, there was no way he could possibly pay it off. And that is what makes verse 27 so remarkable: "And the lord of that slave felt compassion and released him and forgave him the debt."

Now when we read that we think, "Well, the debt was not paid." Right? But it was. In forgiveness the debt is always paid. True, it was not paid by the employee, but it was paid by the king who decided to look on the loss as a bad loan or a shaky investment, rather than the embezzlement that it was. The king had to absorb the loss, and there was no tax write-off. He was out as much as $1 billion, because someone always has to pay. David Augsburger, speaker for "The Mennonite Hour," speaks directly to the point:

> Forgiveness is hard. Especially in a marriage tense with past troubles, tormented by fears of rejection and humiliation, and torn by suspicion and distrust. Forgiveness hurts. Especially when it must be extended to a husband or wife who doesn't deserve it, who hasn't earned it, who may misuse it. It hurts to forgive. Forgiveness costs. Especially in marriage when it means accepting instead of demanding repayment for the wrong done; where it means releasing the other instead of exacting revenge; when it means reaching out in love instead of relinquishing resentments. It costs to forgive.[4]

In cultivating eyes of love—magic eyes, at that—we must be willing to acknowledge that we have been wronged, had our rights trampled on, been insulted and deceived, if we

are to forgive the other person doing all this to us. We must
be willing to pay the price and release the other person,
just as the king released his servant.

To see with magic eyes, we must pay the debt, the price.
What God is asking us to do is to demonstrate to others the
same grace, the same love, the same forgiveness that we
have been granted by Him. Our forgiveness also involved
the paying of a debt; what we owe to God because of our
sins was paid by Jesus Christ's death.

> I was thanking the Father today for His mercy. I began
> listing the sins He'd forgiven. One by one I thanked God
> for forgiving my stumbles and rumbles. My motives were
> pure and my heart was thankful, but my understanding
> of God was wrong. It was when I used the word *remem-*
> *ber* that it hit me.
>
> Remember the time I . . . I was about to thank God for
> another act of mercy. But I stopped. Something was
> wrong. The word *remember* seemed displaced. It was an
> off-key note in a sonata, a misspelled word in a poem. It
> was a baseball game in December. It didn't fit. "Does
> He remember?"
>
> Then *I* remembered. I remembered His words. "And I
> will remember their sins no more."
>
> God doesn't just forgive, He forgets. He erases the
> board. He destroys the evidence. He burns the micro-
> film. He clears the computer.
>
> He doesn't remember my mistakes. For all the things
> He does do, this is one thing He refuses to do. He
> refuses to keep a list of my wrongs. When I ask for
> forgiveness He doesn't pull out a clipboard and say, "But
> I've already forgiven him for that five hundred and six-
> teen times."
>
> He doesn't remember.
>
> "As far as the east is from the west, so far has He
> removed our transgressions from us."
>
> No, He doesn't remember. But I do, you do. You still
> remember. You're like me. You still remember what you
> did before you changed. In the cellar of your heart lurk

the ghosts of yesterday's sins. Sins you've confessed; errors of which you've repented; damage you've done your best to repair.

And though you're a different person, the ghosts still linger. Though you've locked the basement door, they still haunt you. They float to meet you, spooking your soul and robbing your joy. With wordless whispers they remind you of moments when you forgot whose child you were.

That horrid lie.

That business trip you took away from home, that took you *so* far away from home.

The time you exploded in anger.

Those years spent in the hollow of Satan's hand.

That day you were needed, but didn't respond.

That date.

That jealousy.

That habit.

As a result, your spiritual walk has a slight limp. Oh, you're still faithful. You still do all the right things and say all the right words. But just when you begin to make strides, just when your wings begin to spread and you prepare to soar like an eagle, the ghost appears. It emerges from the swamps of your soul and causes you to question yourself.

The ghost spews waspish words of accusation, deafening your ears to the promises of the cross. And it flaunts your failures in your face, blocking your vision of the Son and leaving you the shadow of a doubt.

Now, honestly. Do you think God sent that ghost? Do you think God was teasing when He said, "I will remember your sins no more?" Was He exaggerating when He said He would cast our sins as far as the east is from the west?

Of course you don't. You and I just need an occasional reminder of God's nature, His forgetful nature.

To love conditionally is against God's nature.

You see, God is either the God of perfect grace . . . or He is not God. Grace forgets. Period. He who is perfect love cannot hold grudges. If He does, then He isn't perfect love. And if He isn't perfect love, you might as well put this book down and go fishing, because both of us are chasing fairy tales.

Think about this. If He didn't forget, how could we pray? How could we sing to Him? How could we dare enter into His presence, if the moment He saw us He remembered all our pitiful past? How could we enter His throne room wearing the rags of our selfishness and gluttony? We couldn't.

We are presumptuous not when we marvel at His grace, but when we reject it. And we're sacrilegious not when we claim His forgiveness, but when we allow the haunting sins of yesterday to convince us that God forgives but He doesn't forget.

Do yourself a favor. Purge your cellar. Exorcise your basement. Take the Roman nails of Calvary and board up the door.

And remember . . . He forgot.[5]

But even more than forgetting, forgiveness requires unusual patience with people's faults. The servant pleaded, "Have patience with me" (v. 26). We've seen this word *patience* already in our study of love. It means "a long way from anger." But too often we hit the ceiling with people before we even consider forgiveness. Unresolved anger lies at the root of many unforgiving hearts. And yet, magic eyes cannot coexist for very long with angry eyes.

In interpersonal relationships, people who forgive are always patient people. But in our hurried and harried society, that quality seems to be a diminishing resource. Gail and Gordon MacDonald, who have reason to understand forgiveness, talk about the importance of patience in our lives:

We simply don't like to wait for things, or for growth or development in people. We want each other to change, to mature, to respond in certain ways *instantly*. But sometimes it takes years to develop wisdom, the grace, and the endurance we want to see in one another. Such people-growth cannot happen outside the environment of

patience. Simply put, patience is the willingness to generously give another time and space to grow. Patience
(like love) does not demand; it waits.[6]

Impatient, angry, unforgiving hearts jump all over the mistakes of others. Magic eyes that beam from a heart of love
understand that forgiveness has moved a long distance from
anger, for forgiveness puts up with the mistakes of others.

It was a family treasure, that vase that golden vase
The vase that had belonged to my great-grandmother, to
my grandmother, and now to my mother . . .
And the vase sat on the mantle out of reach of little
fingers.
However, I managed to reach it
I climbed to reach it
I broke it — the family treasure.
Golden pieces of once a family treasure valueless
    that moments before was priceless
And I began to cry,
    then louder in sobs that brought my mother running.
I could hardly get it out:
    I broke the vase . . . the treasure.
And then my mother gave to me a gift:
    A look of relief over her face and
    "Oh, I thought you had been hurt!"
And then she hugged to her the one who had
    just moments before broken the family treasure.
She gave me a gift:
    She made it very clear that
        I was the family treasure.
        I was what was priceless and of great value.
She also made it very clear where her heart was.[7]

Forgiveness requires paying a debt. It insists on patience
with other people's faults. But warming all of that, like the
embers of a fire, is the fact that forgiveness cannot live and
breathe unless we have genuine compassion for the other
person. You can see that in two statements from our story.
"And the lord of that slave felt compassion and released

him and forgave him the debt. . . . Should you not also have
mercy on your fellow slave, even as I had mercy on you?"
(vv. 27, 33)

The verb for *felt compassion* in verse 27 is the strongest
word in Greek to express this feeling. It describes an emotion which moves to the very depths of one's being. Now
the remarkable part about this word is that to a Greek,
using the word in connection with God would have seemed
totally out of place. The Greeks, especially the Stoic philosophers, believed in an emotionless god who was incapable
of pity. In fact, pagan ethics taught that one purpose of life
was to remove all compassion from day-to-day excursions.

Many people today follow this same philosophy, especially
men. Under the guise of being "macho," they have closed the
doorways of their hearts and will not allow compassion to
enter. They refuse to look at others through magic eyes.

How unlike Christ! A key quality in Jesus' life was a
compassion that never stopped, but touched with gentleness everything that He did. In fact, Jesus might have pref-
aced every day's work with the phrase, "I will have compassion." And He could have fallen asleep every night to
the words, "I have had compassion." That lifted Him head
and shoulders above the feelingless gods of the Greeks, for
Jesus Christ entered into people's lives and felt for them,
especially for hurting people who needed forgiveness.

Magic eyes are motivated by compassion and urged on
by mercy. Mercy goes beyond sympathy. It is *sympathy and
compassion in action toward someone in need.* Mercy puts
wheels on compassion. It reaches out, not simply to observe
a need, but to meet the need.

Over a century ago Walt Whitman said, "I do not ask
how the wounded one feels; I, myself, become the wounded one." That's mercy, meeting the need. And when you
look around, you will discover that one of the primary
needs in people's hearts is their need to be forgiven. What
comes from their past haunts them and they see no way of
erasing it. Psychology recognizes this and tries to help peo-

ple deal with the guilt. But in order to deal with it, some say you have to redefine it so that it doesn't exist. But that kind of word play works only in the mind, not in the heart. The guilt still howls every night, every moment the mind is not actively engaged. Millions of people desperately long to know that they are forgiven.

Some years ago, in the city of Boston, lived a well-known Christian gentleman. He was from a well-do-to family and lived in the lap of luxury. This, however, did not dampen his zeal for the Lord and he was known for his great witness and love for God. He married a beautiful woman and for several years they had a happy life together. Then, for some reasons that are not clear, the wife began drinking and soon became a helpless alcoholic. Being part of this prestigious family became too much for her, and one day she wrote a note to her husband. "I cannot live up to the sterling quality of your testimony and I am going to leave, so as not to embarrass you further."

When the husband returned home that day and found the note, he immediately began a network search for his wife. He placed ads in newspapers all over the country. He had pleas for her return aired on radio and television. He sent pictures to various funeral homes. The police and sheriff were called in. Everything anyone could do was done.

One day, several weeks later, he received a phone call from a funeral home saying they thought they had his wife there — she was dead. Leaving quickly, the husband arrived in the other city and identified the woman as his wife.

Leaving her there temporarily, he went out into the city to a monument maker and purchased an expensive stone to her memory. On it he placed only one word — FORGIVEN.

So it is for the Christian. While on earth we do things seemingly without rhyme or reason, and we disappoint the Lord by sinning against Him. But when all is said and done, and we have finished our life here, we don't have to fear. *The monument of the cross stands before us with one word printed on it — forgiven.*

The point of Jesus' story about the king is that we as
believers have experienced that forgiveness and now have
the opportunity of sharing it. Nothing other people can do
to us in any way compares with how we have offended God.
And, since God in Christ has forgiven us the debt we owe
to Him, we must forgive others the debts they owe us.

THE GOD OF FORGIVENESS

Now we need to wrap this all together with some final
observations about forgiveness. The first concerns what
happens to us when we refuse to forgive. "That slave went
out and found one of his fellow-slaves who owed him 100
denarii; and he seized him and began to choke him, saying,
'Pay back what you owe.' So his fellow-slave fell down and
began to entreat him, saying, 'Have patience with me and I
will repay you.' He was unwilling, however, but went and
threw him in prison until he should pay back what was
owed" (Matthew 18:28-30).

The debt this man refused to forgive amounted to a one-
six-hundred-thousandth part of his forgiven debt. Incredibly, he became rigid in his greed and deliberately chose not
to forgive, but to punish. And what happened to him? "And
his lord, moved with anger, handed him over to the torturers until he should repay all that was owed him. So shall
My Heavenly Father also do to you, if each of you does not
forgive his brother from your heart" (vv. 34-35).

What does this mean for us? If we do not forgive, we will
be tormented by our own bitterness and resentment, and
love will exit through the back door screen of our lives. We
all know people who have been hurt by others. But rather
than moving on, they have nursed their grudges. When this
man was tossed into prison, he knew he would die there,
because he could not in his lifetime repay the debt he
owed. And there are people today who have gone to their
graves holding on to an unforgiving and bitter spirit.

My friend, the goal of forgiveness is reconciliation. But sometimes, no matter how you try, reconciliation doesn't work. Parents move away, or they die before you can seek forgiveness, or before they can apologize and seek your forgiveness. Friends move to other parts of the country and you cannot be in touch with them except by letter or phone. Spouses leave you and divorce stalks you and there is no other contact except perhaps in the support check . . . if there is one. There are times then when reconciliation cannot be pursued in a practical, personal way.

In those moments, you must choose by God's grace to forgive and move on, or else be imprisoned by the ghost of resentment. Listen to one person's experience here:

> The first person to benefit from forgiving is always the person who forgives. We purge our heart of the poison someone meanly put there. We lift ourselves from the bilge of hate and dance to the melody of inner healing. We set a prisoner free and discover that the prisoner was us. We create a new beginning for ourselves by unlocking the shackles that otherwise would hold us tight inside a painful past.[8]

Have you unlocked the shackles? If not, other people you run with will notice your behavior and it will not impress. That's what verse 31 says: "So when his fellow-slaves saw what had happened, they were deeply grieved and came and reported to their lord all that had happened." If we hold onto that grudge, if we cling to that bitterness, that is what people will see in our lives and it will hurt them. They will not see anything of the joy of the Lord Jesus Christ, but they're going to see a bitter individual who wants revenge. The world's worst prison is the prison of an unforgiving heart. And in that prison, the pebbles drop into our hearts one by one, and we don't see straight anymore, because our eyesight grows cloudier and darker every day. That's why we must remember that forgiveness is a promise we make, in three ways.

First, forgiveness is a promise that we make *to the individual who has offended us,* in which we say, at least to ourselves, "I will not let my attitude be controlled any longer by this incident. It has been put aside."

Second, forgiveness is a promise *not to pass the hurt on to someone else.* Now, it may be that others know about it, but regardless of that, forgiveness means that no one throws it at the offender again, or holds it over his head, or reminds her of it every time another problem surfaces. It is a promise to drop the matter, leave it in the past and NEVER bring it up again. But you may say, "I do remember it. It hurt so bad! How can I possibly forget?" You can't. Forgiveness does not involve forgetting. Our minds are not made that way.

And here is where the third promise comes in. Forgiveness is a promise to yourself that when your memory goes back to the hurt, *you are not going to dwell on it or nurse it into flame again.* You are promising to repeat your act of forgiveness, no matter how often the memory comes up. And as that begins to take place, you'll notice the change. You'll see it first of all in your eyes . . . *they'll be magic eyes.*

There was once a little hunchback boy in Sunday School who had memorized some Bible verses along with all the other kids in his class. One Sunday evening he was to come up to the front of the church and recite the verses. One cruel youngster, when he saw the little boy stumbling on the stage, yelled out, "Hey, cripple, why don't you get the pack off your back." You could have heard a pin drop as this little boy stopped and dissolved in tears. All of a sudden a man got up and walked down the aisle and came and stood by the boy and put his arm around him. He said, "I don't know what kind of a person would say something like that, but I just want to say that the most courageous person in this room today is this little boy. You see he's my son and I'm proud of him." And he reached down and picked up that little deformed child and carried him back to his seat.

That is exactly what God does for us. In the bruised,

hunchback, broken fashion of our lives we do our best, and then we are rejected and betrayed and we stumble and make a mess of things. And then our Heavenly Father says, "Ah, you're My child. I'm proud of you and I love you."

6
WHEN LOVE REPAIRS

*Let us not become boastful, challenging one
another, envying one another.*

*Brethren, even if a man is caught in any trespass,
you who are spiritual, restore such a one
in a spirit of gentleness; looking to yourselves,
lest you too be tempted.
Bear one another's burdens,
and thus fulfill the law of Christ.*

Galatians 5:26–6:2

Dr. Paul Brand, pioneer medical missionary to lepers, tells the following story:

In my medical career I have never felt more helpless and despairing than at one time in India when I treated a patient who lacked the basic mechanism of healing. A young missionary couple brought in their infant daughter who had been vomiting and showing signs of a blocked intestine. I operated immediately, removing the section of impacted and gangrenous bowel. The parents left delighted and grateful, taking Anne home for post-operative care.

A few days later, the couple returned with their daughter. The mother had noticed the dressings were wet. As I unwrapped the bandages, I could detect the unmistakable odor of intestinal fluid, and indeed, I could see it seeping out of the wound. Feeling embarrassed, I took the baby to the operating room and reopened the incision. Strangely, as I cut through the surface stitches, the wound fell loosely apart. It showed no sign of healing. Similarly, inside the abdominal cavity I found the intestine leaking and unhealed. It did not look diseased or infected, just porous. This time I cut away the edges and made a most meticulous closure using many fine stitches.

A series of operations followed. It soon became clear that the little girl lacked the unifying healing processes that coordinate various cells . . . sewing her intestine was like sewing a rubber balloon: it would always leak, because nothing summoned new living cells to seal up the puncture marks. Repairs lasted a few days, until the stitches ripped through the tissue.

We prayed over Anne's tiny body. I did research on her condition. We gave her nourishment and blood transfusions through her veins . . . but nothing ever healed. The skin flaps refused to adhere, the muscles gaped apart, and intestinal juices sooner or later trickled out between the stitches. Little Anne would lie there with a sweet and trusting smile as we surveyed the damage, and her face would tear at my heart. She grew thinner and thinner. I don't think Anne experienced much pain; she just *quietly faded away.* When the tiny, wasted body was wrapped for burial, I cried in grief and helplessness.

Anne's body lacked the *go-between,* the mechanism that responds to a wound by healing it. She had plenty of [fiber building material] and new cells—her body was using them for growth all over, weaving fiber for tendons and tissue. *Nothing, however informed them that her body was wounded, and that they must rush to the site of injury. No alarms went off alerting one part of the body to another's need.*[1]

There is another body that seems to have the same kind of problem—the body of Christ. Frequently, no one is informed that the body has been wounded, that it is bleeding from injuries. Seemingly, no alarms go off alerting one part of the body to another's need, and so, the broken pieces of people's lives are not mended; no one knows that they must rush to the site of the injury. The result? *Wounded believers just fade away.*

Perhaps that explains, at least in part, why over 15 million Americans now belong to some 500,000 self-help groups. One significant aspect to that statistic is that these people have decided to bypass the traditional avenues of institutional assistance—such as the church—in favor of groups which "deal with people like themselves who have conquered or are trying to solve the problems in their lives."[2] The report implies that the church gives the impression that no one has problems, hurts, injuries or wounds.

Some 15 million Americans have bypassed the church, the body of Christ, because rather than assisting our wounded, we tend to shoot them, and then rinse the blood out of the carpet so no one notices. And as a result, the broken pieces of people's lives are not mended, the wounds are not healed.

WHEN LOVE GETS PRACTICAL

As unfortunate as this is, it is not a new problem. Churches in the first century struggled with the same thing. And so the Apostle Paul, a man with the hide of a rhinoceros but the heart of a lamb, wrote some words of counsel to help them deal with this issue. This passage describes our personal relationships with fellow-believers in the congregation and shows that the filling of the Holy Spirit is not some private, mysterious experience, but works out in our *practical relationships of love* with other people. In other words, the quality of our personal relationships is a measure of our spirituality.

It is all too easy to talk about *love* in an abstract and generic manner. It is infinitely more difficult to come out of the spiritual clouds and actually demonstrate love to others.

When our relationships are going along smoothly, we don't sense any problem. But the test for the quality of our relationships occurs when there *are* problems, when a wound of sin has been inflicted on the body. Here's how Paul says we should respond: "Brethren, even if a man is caught in any trespass, you who are spiritual, restore such a one in a spirit of gentleness; looking to yourselves, lest you too be tempted" (Galatians 6:1).

The best of us slip up, don't we? That's what the word *trespass* means, "slipping on an icy road or a dangerous path." All of us understand that spiritually. You see, Paul is *not* thinking of behavior which so blatantly scoffs at accepted biblical standards that it brings public embarrassment to the church. He is not referring to someone whose life is *characterized* by sin. What Paul is talking about here is someone who is marching with the army of Christ, whose heart has been transformed, but who finds him/herself caught, to the surprise of everyone, in a sin. A trespass is *not a settled course of action,* but *an isolated incident* which makes the person who does it feel guilty. He is not proud of what he has done; in fact, he'd give his eyeteeth to be able to repeat the down, to go to the plate and bat again. He is truly sorry and repentant.

Spiritual failures are like skipping stones on a pond, except that they never seem to sink out of sight. They just keep skimming across the surface of our lives forever. And when that happens to us, we feel apart and cut off, we feel wounded, injured, guilty and in need of help.

Paul knew that when we have fallen, when we have evidenced weakness, when we feel like a spiritual failure, when the foghorn of guilt makes us want to run from its blast . . . at that moment we need *outside* help. We need someone to come alongside and bandage our wounds and pick us up.

That's why I want you to notice what Paul does *not* say. He does not say, "Brethren, even if a man is caught in any trespass, you who are spiritual *reveal* it to everyone." But that happens, doesn't it? We sometimes give an incident wide publicity because we inwardly enjoy punishing others, or because we can then boast about how much better we are than the one who has fallen. Nor does Paul say, "*Rejoice* over the one who sinned." That happens too. Some Christians think the only way they can look good is to make others look bad. Finally, Paul does not advise that we *reject* that person. He talks about *restoring*.

To a fisherman of Paul's day, *restore* meant to mend the nets. To a soldier, *restore* meant being equipped for battle again. He has lost a battle, but he doesn't have to lose the war. Someone needs to get him back on his feet again.

But the best picture of the verb *restore* is a medical one. The word was used to picture the work of a surgeon removing a growth from a person's body, of repairing a wound, or in setting of a fractured or dislocated bone. The word stresses cure, not punishment. The tense of the verb here is present, meaning this is a repeated, continuing action. Restoring people is not a one-time deal. It happens over and over again.

When it doesn't, when we rejoice, reveal, or reject, we are ignoring the alarms that have gone off alerting us that another part of the body needs our help, our care. And the wound enlarges, the pain intensifies, and the blood continues to flow.

When a believer has a broken bone spiritually, that weakened limb hurts the rest of the body. Our responsibility is not to get a crowbar and pipe wrench and make it worse. Our responsibility is to set the broken bone, so that the limb can be used again. We are to restore and help the person get going again. The great reformer, Martin Luther, has such a marvelous word for us on this text:

> Therefore if (you) see any brother cast down and afflicted by occasion of sin which he has committed, *run* unto him, and *reaching* out your hand, *raise* him up again, *comfort* him with sweet words and *embrace* him with motherly arms. As for those that be hard-hearted and obstinate, which without fear continue careless in their sins, rebuke them sharply. But on the other side (as I said), they that be overtaken with any sin, and are heavy and sorrowful for the fault which they have committed, (they) must be raised up. . . .[3]

Charles Haddon Spurgeon, a great British preacher of another era, had a brother, Thomas, who had weak ankles. Frequently their father would be very unhappy with Thomas for falling down. Finally, the father warned him that he would be whipped if he came home again showing signs of having fallen.

Years later, Charles Spurgeon reminded his father of that threat. "Yes, it was so," said his father, "and Thomas was completely cured from that time." To which Charles replied, "Ah, so you thought, yet it was not so, for he had many a tumble afterwards, but I always managed to wash his knees, and to brush his clothes off, so as to remove all traces of his falls."[4]

There are three elements that embrace our restoration of others. First, we help the person see their own sin, if they haven't already. Second, we then lead them to confess it to God, to repent of it, if they have not. Third, we then encourage the person to move on in God's grace. And isn't that exactly what our God does for each of us . . . over and over and over again?

You've all seen geese flying in a V formation. Scientists have discovered why they do that. As each bird flaps its wings, it creates an uplift for the bird immediately following. By flying in a V they add 70 percent flying range to their travel. When they honk, it is to encourage the one in front to keep up speed. If a goose gets sick or is wounded by a gunshot and falls out of formation, two other geese follow him down to help and protect him. They stay with him until he is able to fly, or until he is dead, and then they launch out on their own or with another formation in order to catch up to their original group.

When the cry for help comes from a fellow believer who has fallen, or has been shot down and lies wounded, our assignment is break stride, reduce our flight speed, and look to restore that person.

WHEN IT IS TIME TO RESTORE

But before we can restore, before we can hear the alarms and rush to the site of the injury, we need to be aware of positive and negative *prerequisites* for the restoring process.

• The first reminds of what WE SHOULD NOT DO during the restoring process. "Let us not become boastful, challenging one another, envying one another" (Galatians 5:26).

Verse 26 really belongs to chapter 6. We could read the verses this way: "Let us not become boastful, challenging one another, envying one another, brethren, even if a man is caught in any trespass." You see, when people are down, when they have been caught in sin, and they are in spiritual and emotional pain—we must not come at them with a superior or arrogant attitude. The word *boastful* describes someone who has an opinion of himself that is empty or false. This person is cherishing a self-illusion that is just plain conceited.

When you are boastful and then you encounter someone who is wounded, you tend to view yourself as superior. You disdain them and tend to treat them as if they had the plague. What's worse is to challenge or provoke them. It implies that you are so sure of your superiority that you want to demonstrate it. So, you challenge the fallen person—go after them verbally, remind them of how awful their behavior was. You might say things like, "How could you do that?" or "What's wrong with you? I thought you were a Christian," or "Why can't you get your life together? When are you going to grow up anyway?"

The insidious part of such attack is that often it is rooted not only in arrogance, but in feelings of envy. You watch someone from a distance and see them succeed; you observe how popular they are, how people always seem to respond favorably to them. They never seem to lack... don't appear to make any mistakes, and you compare that to your experience and find you don't measure up. So you *invent* a false image for yourself and then wait for them to mess up. And when they do, you pounce, boast, challenge. *But you don't restore, don't mend the wound.* And people bleed to death.

In the kind of operating room most churches run, people don't survive very long, because there are no life-support systems, nobody is responding to the alarms, nobody is willing to extend God's grace.

● Fortunately, there are some physicians of the soul in every congregation who do operate differently. They're described with the second and third prerequisites found in verse 1 of chapter 6: "Brethren, even if a man is caught in any trespass, you who are spiritual, restore such a one in a spirit of gentleness; looking to yourselves, lest you too be tempted."

The word *spiritual* refers to mature Christians whose life and conduct are dominated by the Spirit of Christ. Paul is not talking here about "super saints," but about people who are spiritual, in the sense that the fruit of God's Spirit is evident in their lives. It doesn't matter whether they are officially in leadership positions in a church, whether anyone notices them, or whether they have been trained, but simply, is the fruit of God's spirit visible? It is significant that heading the list of the fruit of the Spirit in verse 22 of chapter 5 of Galatians is love.

The test of spirituality is not how many verses of the Bible you have memorized. It is not how many years ago you became a member of the church, or where or when you were baptized or confirmed. It is not even the length of time you have been a Christian. The *test of spirituality* here is your readiness to restore the wounded, your desire to do surgery so that they can function once again. The way you respond to someone who sins indicates whether or not you are spiritual. Do you have a desire to help? To want to offer a hand and not a fist? To extend an arm around the shoulder rather than a kick in the teeth?

What's the score, Lord? *My score.* I know I lost my temper today and there was that half-truth on top of the sting of envy. But consider, Lord, that I went to choir practice when I was really too tired, and that cake I baked for a neighbor, plus the selfless way I've served on that committee *all year.* Doesn't that at least even up the score?

You say the score is *nothing* to *one,* Lord? *Nothing* I can do by myself will earn Your favor? And there's only *one* way to win? Through Jesus, Your perfect Son who died for me to give me all His goodness. So the score is in Your favor. *But I win!* [5]

When we remember the work of Christ, there will come into the restoration arena an attitude of gentleness. The word *gentleness* means "humility and courtesy." It is born out of a sense of our own weakness and tendency toward sin. But more than that, gentleness indicates that we must not have an attitude of haste or impatience in the process of restoration. *Restoration takes time.* And we cannot impose our schedule on it.

But beyond that, gentleness does not enjoy the pain that occurs when the broken bones are reset, or when the wounds are disinfected and bandaged. It does not feel an inward satisfaction when the offending person suffers because of their mistake. Restorers approach the process gently and with encouragement.

George Washington Carver spoke of gentleness this way: "How far you go in life depends on your being tender with the young, compassionate with the aged, sympathetic with the striving, and tolerant of the weak and the strong. Because someday in life you will have been all of these."[6]

And perhaps it was that kind of understanding that prompted Paul to add the final phrase of verse 1 of chapter 6, as part of the restoring process: "looking to yourselves, lest you too be tempted." Paul reminds us that we restore others partly for our own sake, because someday we also might find ourselves falling and in need of a bandage. When we see another Christian stumble we are often tempted to think, "Look what happened to her. I would never have done that!" *But how do we know that?*

What happened to the other guy can happen to us. Each of us has the same potential to fall, to stumble. So Paul reminds us to look inside ourselves. The verb he uses means more than just a quick glance; it involves a careful consideration. It is a word used for looking at a target before releasing a shot. In fact, our word "scope" comes from this word. Paul says, "Start looking at your own life, scope it out, and realize what could happen to you." Dr. John Stott so perceptibly observes at this point:

> If we walked by the Spirit we would love one another more, and if we loved one another more . . . we would not shrink from seeking to restore a brother who has fallen into sin. Further, if we obeyed this . . . instruction as we should, much unkind gossip would be avoided, more serious backsliding prevented, the good of the Church advanced and the name of Christ glorified.[7]

WHEN THERE ARE BURDENS TO BEAR

When we fall, we need help. When the alarms go off, and our hearts scream with pain, that's when we look for someone to demonstrate love to us. And that's the last word Paul has for us in verse 2: "Bear one another's burdens, and thus fulfill the law of Christ."

Some Christians are not interested in bearing burdens. They find it more enjoyable to increase them, by being harder on other people than on themselves. But that is not the advice of our text. The word *burdens* refers to mistakes and sins that press in on a person like a vise and produce sorrow and guilt. Burden-bearing is the mutual, loving participation in the other person's guilt; it is a weeping with those who weep; it is sympathy when the pressure to fall to pieces is great.

But let's think through the implications of this. It is one thing to share the burdens of others when we can do so standing firm on our own feet, stretching out a hand, but remaining unentangled and independent. It is quite another thing to accept a share in the shame and the consequence of another's sin and stand beside them in the mess they have made, and even carry some of the loss of respect—because not eveyone in the church will appreciate your desire to restore. Some people recoil from the idea of burden-bearing. They are much happier attacking, criticizing, condemning, or just staying detached. Don't let those people deter *you* from restoring the wounded soldiers, for as you restore, you "fulfill the law of Christ."

The law of Christ is essentially no different from the command, "Love one another." And that command was considered by Jesus to be the greatest of the commandments in terms of personal relationships. Loving one another as Christ loved us may not lead us to some heroic, flashy, spectacular action, but to the much more mundane, routine, but life-saving ministry of burden-bearing.

But it is not always enough just to pick someone up. You may have to keep holding them up. You may need to put your life up against theirs, support them, pray with and for them, keep in close contact, and help them bear their burdens. The law of Christ is fulfilled when you love my brother or sister enough to get involved and give real help with their problems.

Remember Dr. Brand's story about little Anne. Nothing informed her healthy cells that her body was wounded and that they should rush to the site of the injury. No alarms alerted one part of the body to another's need. In the body of Christ, very often no one is informed that the body has been wounded, that it is bleeding internally from a person's hurt. Seemingly, no alarms go off alerting one part of the body to another's need. And, as a result, the broken pieces of people's lives are not mended.

Dale Galloway's book *Dream a New Dream* is about his broken life that was patched up by the grace and love of God. In it he tells this story:

> A little boy moved into a new neighborhood. He was quiet and shy. His name was Chad. One day he came home and said, "You know what Mom, Valentine's Day is coming and I want to make a valentine for everyone in my class. I want them to know that I love them."

His mother's heart sank, as she thought, "I wish he wouldn't do that" because every afternoon she would watch all the children coming home from school and they would be laughing and hanging on to one another, books under their arms—all except Chad. He always walked behind them. She thought however that she would go along with him, so glue and paper and crayons were purchased and for three weeks he painstakingly made thirty-five valentines. When the day came to deliver the valentines he was so excited, this was his day. He stacked those valentines under his arm and ran out the door. His mother thought, "It's going to be a tough day for Chad, I'll bake some cookies and have some milk ready for him when he comes home from school; maybe that will help ease the pain since he won't be getting very many valentines."

That afternoon she had the warm cookies and the milk out on the table. She went over to the window and scratched a little of the frost off the glass and looked out. Sure enough, here came the big gang of children, laughing, valentines under their arms, they had really done well. And there was her Chad. Coming up behind he was walking faster than usual and she thought, "Bless his heart, he's ready to break into tears." His arms are empty. He doesn't have a valentine.

He came into the house and she said, "Darling, Mom has some warm cookies and milk for you. Just sit down."

But his face was all aglow. He just marched right by her and all he could say was, "Not a one, not a single one. I didn't forget one. They all know I love 'em."[8]

7
HOW LOVE
REALLY CARES

But we proved to be gentle among you,
as a nursing mother tenderly cares
for her own children. Having thus a fond affection
for you, we were well-pleased to impart to you
not only the gospel of God
but also our own lives,
because you had become very dear to us.

For you recall, brethren, our labor and hardship,
how working night and day
so as not to be a burden to any of you,
we proclaimed to you the gospel of God.

1 Thessalonians 2:7-9

In his fine book, *Letters to a Young Doctor,* Dr. Richard Selzer tells this story:

I had a friend who looked like an elf — the same triangle of a face in which every bone was visible. The same dark eyes, sharp nose and pointed elf's ears. His name was Gerald and he was 6 inches shy of 5 feet, and eel-thin. His skin was devoid of color — white and bloodless. His hair was straight and unevenly planted. Each of his ears was missing a ridge of cartilage, which gave them a thin, unrolled look. Gerald had a hollow, strained voice, as though he were shouting into a wind. His r's, w's and l's were in some disarray.

"I can't wead," he said. "I wike to wook at pickchews."

For twelve years Gerald scraped trays in the hospital cafeteria. Dressed in soiled white pants and a white shirt, and with a great paper cylinder resting on his ears, he stood behind the tiered shelf where the trays were stowed. He would pull the trays in toward himself, remove the dirty dishes and scrape the garbage into a trash can. I don't know how it was that Gerald and I began to have lunch together every Tuesday. As Emily Dickinson said, "It was just a happen."

Gerald knew and remembered everything about me —

what I had eaten for lunch the previous Tuesday, where I was supposed to be at any given time, what operations I performed — everything. He had his sources. Such details are unimportant to you and me, but to a [person who loves] they are crucial.

"What did I eat last week?" I would ask him. "I don't want to get the same things."

"Clam chowder, brussel sprouts, and cherry pie," he would recite, and his face would brim with the joy of such knowledge. By just such intimacies had Gerald gained his power over me.

When Gerald wasn't worrying about his health, he was smiling. And he could be easily distracted from his hypochondria. He adored presents and accepted anything, no matter how meager, with a joy that passeth all understanding. I gave him everything I carried that was not essential, in order to collect for myself another [drop] of Gerald's joy. One day Gerald came to my office for a visit. Just dropped in. I gave him a pair of my shoes that I had just had resoled. "Sit down there," I told him, pointing to the swivel chair behind my desk. He was thrilled. I knelt and unlaced his shoes and slipped them off. I put my shoes on him. They were a vast acreage about his narrow, raccoon feet.

"How do they feel?"

"Good," he said. "They feel real good!"

"They're not for work," I said. "They're just for you, at home."

"No," he said. "Not for work."

"You're following in my footsteps," I told him.

"I'm wearing your shoes," he said.

"I have to go to work now," I said.

Gerald smiled and clomped out, barely able to hold his new shoes on his feet.

Gerald loved to be told a story. Best received was a long account of a painful illness terminating in near death. The hero was always a surgeon who operated on the patient just in time. Gerald would sit through my [longest] stories, rocking back and forth. "You are a dear man," he would say when I finished. "You never change."

It was the closest Gerald came to confessing his love.

I did not see Gerald for a month because I had under-taken to teach a noon hour class. Nor did I see him the next month because I was on vacation. When I came back, it was to find that Gerald had been admitted to the hospital with pneumonia the week before. Within three days, he was dead. I went to visit his mother. "He missed you," she said. "He was pining."

I learned that you must never run out on an elf, or hurt an elf's feelings. To an elf, such a wound is invari-ably fatal.[1]

I believe that the Apostle Paul would have quickly identi-fied with that story, especially as he thought back to a church where he had spent time, in the city of Thessa-lonica.

In many ways, he was deeply attached to the Christians in that place, even though he had left their city some two and one-half years earlier. And although his departure from them had been forced, he was still concerned about his friends. He hoped that his premature leaving had not hurt them, that they were not *pining* for him. And despite the negative critics who still lived in that place, Paul's heart stayed with these people. They were for him "the stuff that dreams are made of." They were his "Geralds," if you will. And as he looked across time and space to his friends in Thessalonica, his heart of love leaped to them. They were quite literally his heart and soul's desire.

HOW DEEPLY DO I CARE?

In fact, that is precisely what Paul says to them: "Having then a fond affection for you, we were well-pleased to im-part to you not only the Gospel of God but also our own lives, because you had become very dear to us" (1 Thessa-lonians 2:8). In these words, Paul reveals a most attractive warmth from deep within himself. He was at times a man

of feeling and a gentle person. His very language here
expresses a warmth not often linked with Paul. He sometimes reminds us of a cross between Clint Eastwood and
John Wayne, but we don't often see him in a sensitive
mold. His words *fond affection* mean "to long for someone,
as for an old friend." The Greek word describes a grieved
parent's deep longing to once again hold a child who has
died. In fact, this word expressed affection shown in a nursery—so that it is a term of sensitivity and warmth. It's a
word with embers around it.

But Paul doesn't stop with that, for he tells his friends
that his delight was not restricted to sharing the Gospel
with them—as important as that was, his delight went beyond that, to sharing his own life, literally "his soul." The
sense is "his heart—or the depth of his being." He was
willing to give all of himself to these people.

We can tell how far we have risen in the scale of life by
asking ourselves one question: "How wisely and how deeply do I care?" To be Christian should mean that we are
sensitized. Christians are to be people who care. No one
can come into authentic contact with Jesus Christ without
beginning to care.

Do you know the people who age the fastest? Those who
are concerned with themselves and getting on in their life,
who are totally unconcerned with others. Yet the youngest
people I've ever met are those concerned with other people's lives, no matter what their age.

I believe Paul was reassuring his friends that although
his critics in the city of Thessalonica said he was out to use
people and that he didn't care for them, that, in fact, the
opposite was true—his heart longed to see them again because there was a deep bond between them.

He reminds them that they are "very dear" to him. This
comes from the Greek *agape,* the word for love we have
been wrestling with. Paul is stressing his unconditional love
for these people. He wants them to understand that no
matter what they hear from his critics, he loves them with-

out strings, without conditions. He didn't blow into town to say, "I will show love to you IF . . ."

That is how Paul's heart beat. But sometimes, despite his desire to care, he didn't always show it. Even the best of hearts don't always translate their caring onto the pages of people's lives. Sometimes you must read between the lines to see that love, but that is because none of us is perfect. Our desire to express sensitivity and caring may be there, but it just doesn't always come out right.

And yet how easy it is for us to feel offended and upset by those who don't "turn on their heart light" for us in the way we expect, even when a person or group has demonstrated love over the long haul. It's ironic that sometimes those of us who criticize and complain about people not caring for us are, in our criticism and complaining, guilty of not caring for them.

It's easy to misread hearts. But how much better to try to sense someone's heartbeat and give them the positive benefit of the doubt, allowing them room to grow and also realizing that we may never personally experience their heart the way we want to.

Dr. Donald Grey Barnhouse, the great Philadelphia preacher from the middle part of our century offers this understanding of Paul:

> The Apostle Paul had a . . . universal love toward all those who had believed in the Lord Jesus Christ, [but] . . . there seems to be every indication in the [New Testament] that Paul knew he was considered HARD by those to whom he preached. Alone in his own heart he must have longed for the SOFTNESS of the nature of the disciple John. When John told Christians that he loved them, they all answered warmly to his personality and felt themselves beloved of John. [Yet] we know that some people did not like Paul. He hit too hard . . . his blows were sledgehammer blows. There may well have been those who came to him and said, "Paul, show a little more love. . . . " Temperamentally and psychologi-

cally, he was unable to show it. There is a little of John in me and more of Paul.

There may be many Christians who have been accused of pride, or arrogance, who know deep down in their hearts that they are seeking . . . to have the Lord Jesus Christ magnified in their [life]. They love with an intensity that hurts [but] which demonstrates itself in a hardness of outward attitude, although at the same time, like Paul, they may say, "I LOVE."[2]

You have people in your life who are "the stuff that dreams are made of " — Geralds, if you will. As you walk through the hallways of your memory, their images are framed on the walls of your mind. And they are and continue to be "your heart and soul's desire." And sometimes they know that. There are times when the message flows from you loud and clear, and they can't miss it. But there are other times, when even though your heart is shouting your love, that the message cannot quite emerge but seems to echo off into a canyon or gets stuck in your throat. Those for whom you desperately want to express care miss it . . . unless they are special people who understand your heart and accept you.

HOW OPEN IS MY HEART?

Having made allowances for our humanity, we now need to look at ways to increase our ability to give our hearts away. Even a closed heart can begin to unfold ever so slowly. We begin by remembering that love involves hard work. We must remember that love is something we are called to do, and that love requires commitment, concern, and concentration if it is to begin to move out of our hearts. That was true for Paul, who illustrates love with the picture of a nursing mother: "We proved to be gentle among you, as a nursing mother tenderly cares for her own children" (v. 7).

● This picture shows a special effort to protect and to

provide for needs, even to the point of great personal sacrifice. This love is demonstrated in *gentleness* and *tenderness* with people.

In fact, *gentle* refers primarily to sensitivity and kindness. And although Paul uses the word in the context of a mother-child relationship, it was used in other places for the relationship between an employer and employees; a supervisor and staff, and a father with his children. It is a term that encircles all our relationships, for they are to be marked with gentleness.

Certainly that is the emphasis behind the picture of a nursing mother. Her love for her baby is a *tender* love. And Paul is reminding his friends that the love he demonstrated toward them was just as tender and unconditional as the love a mother has for her newborn child.

Although Paul uses the illustration of a nursing mother, he is not speaking just to women. He is describing *his own* relationship with these people. I think that if we were reading this for the first time, not knowing that a man wrote it, we might be tempted to assign the authorship to a woman, because somehow the virtues of gentleness and tenderness do not sound very masculine.

But when we think that way, we fail to understand that true strength always reveals itself in gentleness and courtesy. Somewhere along the line, many of us have come to believe that gentle people get nowhere, because everyone ignores them or steamrolls them; that it is the tough, the overbearing, snarly types who succeed, but that weaklings go to the wall. We seem to have bought into "The Commandments of Masculinity."

He shall not cry.
He shall not display weakness.
He shall not need affection or gentleness or warmth.
He shall comfort but not desire comforting.
He shall be needed but not need.
He shall touch but not be touched.
He shall be steel not flesh.

He shall be invisible in his manhood.
He shall stand alone.[3]

This idea is so hard for some of us to fight off. We just aren't programmed toward love and gentleness. We choke even on the words and find it difficult to relate to them. But we must.

> "I love you." These words have enormous power. Yet, these words are too often so difficult for many men to utter—toward lovers, children, friends, parents, brothers, and sisters. Why? Often because the words are a commitment to caring. Often, because of a fear of feeling and conveying that feeling to a loved one and the sense of open vulnerability this may bring. Often because of the destructive confusion in our society that this kind of expression is less than masculine and may indicate the beginning of being too feeling and less than masterful.
>
> I cannot stress enough the remedial value of these words—how much further they go than material gifts of any kind.
>
> In saying these words we are experiencing, expressing, and asserting the richest, most serious, and important aspect of ourselves. This hugely enhances healthy, emotional self-growth and is evidence of adult investment of emotions in another human being.
>
> This is also an affirmation that we realize loving is at least as important as being loved.
>
> The words "I love you" are an affirmation of active feelings about the other person. In a healthy, long relationship, both are there—being loved and loving.[4]

But, think with me a little longer concerning the image of a mother tenderly caring for her baby. Implicit in that care is the *total acceptance* of the baby. The infant doesn't have to perform to enjoy the love of its mother, nor does it have to look good to be smothered with care. Regardless of performance or appearance, the mother loves her baby. You don't hear too many mothers of newborns saying, "All right baby, I'll change three dirty diapers a day, but that's it," or

"Look, if you want me to love you, you got to know that I will tolerate being awakened only once in the night. Got that?" or, "I love you, but I'm really disappointed with your hair color. If we could just use a little Clairol. . . ." Regardless of performance or appearance, there is love.

This is important, because so much of our love for others is determined by externals. They need to dress at a level we feel good about, work in the proper field according to our standards, and live in an acceptable neighborhood, whether uptown or downtown. Some who are desperate for love will fake those externals in order to be loved.

How sad. Real love is given without expectation. If you love truly, then you have no choice but to believe and hope that your love will be returned, but you have no guarantees. Jesus Christ demonstrated love supremely by dying for our sins, yet there was no guarantee that everyone would respond to Him. If you wait to love until you are certain of receiving equal love in return, you may wait forever. I love the perspective Richard Halverson shared in the U.S. Senate some time ago:

> Love is never wasted. It may not get the results or the reaction expected. But it is never wasted. In fact, love that expects positive reaction or results is *something less than love.* Love never makes demands. Love only gives, and it does not cease giving when there is no return. The true lover does not require the beloved to meet any conditions. True love is unconditional. The perfect Lover devoted Himself totally to others . . . and they crucified Him.[5]

Paul would concur. If ever anyone was assaulted and attacked because he cared, it was Paul. Yet, he reminds us that that is the better way.

● When you give your heart away, it is often through *gentleness* and *tenderness;* but you can also give your heart away through *tireless efforts* on behalf of others. Verse 9 brings this to our attention: "For you recall, brethren, our labor and hardship, how working night and day so as not to be a burden to any of you, we proclaimed to you the Gospel of God."

Paul and Silas worked at night as well as during the day while in this city preaching the Gospel of Christ. It is likely that Paul supported himself at his trade of tentmaking. In other churches, Paul did not hesitate to ask for financial help. But not here. There was a unique relationship. These people as a group were hurting and he knew it was tough, so he lifted the financial burden by working constantly.

It must have been very difficult for him to find time for all of this and not break down under the load, yet, somehow he did. The interesting part of this, however, is that he is still talking more as a nursing mother than as a hard-driving father.

After all, who is it that gets up in the middle of the night to feed the baby? Who stays up all night when the kids are sick? Who camps out by the washer and dryer and folds clothes until ready to scream? Why, *it is the father, of course!*

No, no! It's Mother. And even if Dad does help . . . there is still a difference. When Mom is there, tenderness is dominant. With Dad, it's often irritation and impatience. Dad slides into the scene with statements like, "I don't care if your arm's broken! The game's not over yet . . . get up and act like a man," or "Don't you know its 2 A.M.? What do you mean, you're sick? Talk to your mother!"

But for Mother, no price is too high. Yet there is a price! Paul uses the word *labor*, meaning "work that wearies us . . . that tires us out." When you give your heart away in love to others through ministry, you often feel wrung out.

You may identify with that, if your ministry to people wearies you. You give them your heart and then some, and with every heartbeat you seem to be more tired and less appreciated. You wish you could get up just *one* morning and feel rested.

In verse 9, Paul also says that he experienced hardship, a word that refers to the trouble and pain of difficult work. It suggests struggling in a ministry to overcome difficulties. Implicit in the picture is sacrifice for the benefit of someone else. When you desire to give your heart away in love, that devotion must pulse through your veins. John Henry Jowett stated it well: "Ministry that costs nothing, accomplishes nothing." But I would suggest that ministry that costs nothing is not really ministry at all.

When you desire to give your heart to people, it will involve personal sacrifice on your behalf. And the finest way Paul could illustrate that idea was to think of a mother who often ministers largely behind the scenes, unnoticed. Just as some of you do and will do in the future, as you give your heart away.

That was the way it was for Paul. Amid the spotlight of his public ministry there were some very quiet, behind-the-scenes ministries that received no press. Perhaps his strongest critics who shouted of his uncaring heart never knew about those times, those people, those moments when he gave his heart and soul away at great personal cost.

Some people appear on the surface to be distant, not involved with others. But if we could sweep the corners of their lives, we would see their hearts given away, maybe even broken in the process. If you are one of these people, *don't stop.* Please, don't stop. When you think you can't go on, when you are so tired you want to sleep forever, when your ministry to people in behalf of Jesus Christ seems so insignificant, so unnoticed, so unappreciated, so costly, so sacrificial in comparison with results, *remember Paul's heart!*

> Hast thou no scar? No hidden scar on foot or side or hand? I hear thee sung as mighty in the land, I hear them hail thy bright ascendant star: Hast thou no scar? Hast thou no wound? Yet I was wounded by the archers, spent,
>   Leaned me against the tree to die, and rent by ravening beasts that compassed me, I swooned: Hast thou no wound? No wound? No scar? Yet as the master shall the servant be, and pierced are the feet that follow Me; but

thine are whole. Can you have followed far who has no
wound, no scar?[6]

You ask, "But is it ever appreciated? Does it ever have any
positive results?" *Yes, it does.* You cannot give your heart
away and not ultimately see results. In verse 6 of the next
chapter, we see that Timothy has come to the city of Corinth, where Paul is writing this letter, to bring Paul a report
on the Christians in Thessalonica. Here is his report: "But
now that Timothy has come to us from you, and has
brought us good news of your faith and love, and that you
always think kindly of us, longing to see us just as we also
long to see you, for this reason, brethren, in all our distress
and affliction we were comforted about you through your
faith" (1 Thessalonians 3:6-7).

Can you hear the catch in his voice? Can you feel the hot
tears of relief and gratitude. Now Paul knew that his
friends, his "Geralds," were fine. His ministry had paid off,
and they loved him back.

Let's never stop ministering, sharing our lives with gentleness and tenderness. May we see the eternal value of
tireless, sacrificial ministry in the lives of people and carry
on.

> Bad luck—the light turned red, and I was trapped stand-
> ing at the corner. I prayed for it to change quickly.
>   "Can I have something for my file, mister?" he asked.
>   This one was a crazy—no doubt about it. The grimy
> box under his arm gave him away immediately. Crazies
> always carry something, usually a shopping bag with
> handles. They can be unstable, but this guy looked pretty
> safe.
>   "Sorry, no money." I had repeated the old lie so often
> it came out automatically.
>   "Have you got anything for my file?" he repeated.
>   Slowly the message sank through. I fished in my
> pocket, pulled out a brochure and handed it to him.
>   "No!" he shouted. Then, almost pathetically, he fin-
> ished, "I don't have a file for that."

I took it back and turned away. *Come on light—change.* I stepped over the curb to look for a break in traffic.

"I'm Howard," he said. "What's your name?"

"Mark." One syllable was all the information I intended to give.

I chanced a quick look to see what he was doing. He had a pencil in one hand and was stooping to pick up a piece of paper. Just then the light changed, and I took off.

A few days later, I was walking the same route when I noticed an ambulance parked outside a dingy alley. I joined the crowd of onlookers to see what had happened.

Two attendants in white jackets wheeled their stretcher out of the alley. It was the crazy.

His face was showing, so I knew he wasn't dead. But as the attendants shut the door, I could tell by their conversation that he wouldn't stay uncovered for long.

A policeman questioned some of the people in the crowd, but received no answers. Nobody seemed to care that much, not even the cop. It was just a little added excitement on an otherwise dull day.

The cop raised his voice and asked, "Did anyone know this guy?"

Nobody answered. Finally, I volunteered. "His name is Howard."

The people around me backed away—as if my knowing the crazy's name made me a crazy, too. The cop came over and began to pump me for more information.

"His name is Howard. That's all I know, sir."

"Thank you for your help . . . Oh, by the way—would you take this for me?" He reached down and picked up the crazy's box.

He shoved the box into my hands and walked away before I could say anything.

Why would I want some guy's garbage? I thought.

I looked around for a trash can, but I knew I couldn't just toss the box. Maybe it was the stories of misers who had thousands of dollars yet lived like bums, or perhaps even a slightly misguided sense of loyalty to the human race. Whatever it was, I opened the box.

I was disappointed. I saw nothing but old clothes and one file folder.

No wonder this guy didn't have a file for my brochure. I guess even crazies are into specialization.

I pulled out the file and dumped the rest of the stuff. Then I noticed the crude printing on the folder: "FRIENDS." I opened it and looked inside. It held only one small scrap of paper. On it was written, "Mark."[7]

8
WHEN IT IS HARD
TO LOVE

You are witnesses, and so is God,
how devoutly and uprightly and blamelessly
we behaved toward you believers;
just as you know how we were exhorting
and encouraging and imploring each one of you
as a father would his own children,
so that you may walk in a manner
worthy of the God who calls you
into His own kingdom and glory.

1 Thessalonians 2:10-12

David Niven, in *The Oxford Book of Military Anecdotes*, relates this true story from World War II about a British officer driving through Germany in the first days after the German surrender. Try to place yourself in this story as the British officer explains in his own words what happened next:

I passed a farm wagon headed for the village. I glanced casually at the two men sitting up behind the horse. Both wore typical farmer headgear and sacks were thrown over their shoulders, protecting them from a light drizzle. We were just past them when something made me slam on the brakes and back up. I was right! The man who was not driving was wearing field boots. I slipped out from behind the wheel, pulled my revolver from its holster and told the corporal to cover me with his Tommy gun.

I gestured to the men to put their hands over their heads and told them in fumbling German to produce their papers. "I speak English," said the one with the field boots. "This man has papers—I have none."

"Who are you?" I asked. He told me his name and rank—General. "We are not armed," he added, as I hesitated. I motioned them to lower their hands. "Where are you coming from, sir?"

He looked down at me. I had never seen such utter weariness, such blank despair on a human face before. He passed a hand over the stubble of his chin. "BERLIN," he said quietly.

"Where are you going, sir?"

He looked ahead down the road towards the village and closed his eyes. "Home," he said, almost to himself. "It's not far now . . . only . . . one more kilometer." I didn't say anything. He opened his eyes again and we stared at each other. We were quite still for a long time. Then I said, "Go ahead, sir," and added ridiculously, "Please, cover up your boots." Almost as though in pain, he closed his eyes and raised his head. Then, with sobbing intakes of breath, he covered his face with both hands and they drove on . . . to home.[1]

In the midst of the rubble and anguish of a world war, where toughness, ruthlessness, and stoicism were advantages simply for the sake of survival, that incident seems almost out of place, as if transported from a softer era. Yet it suggests that behind even the harshest exterior, there is the capacity within each of us to give our hearts away in love to others.

LOVING IN DIFFICULT TIMES

Certainly that was true in the life of the crusty Apostle Paul. As he inked out the New Testament Book of 1 Thessalonians, he did so from a context of some pain. The seriousness of the verses before us indicate that Paul was dealing with accusations being used by opponents to slander and damage his reputation and to turn people away from him and the church. It was intense enough that Paul appealed to God and to the believers in the church to validate his ministry, to applaud his efforts of sincerity, to stand as witnesses in his defense. The point is that in the midst of some very difficult circumstances which could easily have turned Paul inward and bitter, he was still able to care for people and to extend his love. Perhaps 1 Thessalonians 2:8 summarizes that love best . . . "Having a fond affection for you, we were well-pleased to impart to you not only the Gospel of God but also our own lives, because you had become very dear to us."

In a crucible of stress and difficulty, many of us respond with the mechanism of defense. Robert Jay Lifton, who studied the survivors of Hiroshima and other disasters, calls that approach "psychic numbing." When our feelings are overwhelmingly painful or unpleasant, we have the capacity to anesthetize ourselves, to simply tune out the pain, and become insensitive to those around us.[2]

That same potential was available to Paul, but verse 8 assures us that is not the course he took. He is reassuring his friends that although his critics say that he is out to use people, that he doesn't care for them, in fact, the opposite is true. His heart longs to see them because there is a deep bond between them. That is how Paul's heart beat.

And for those of us who claim the name of Christ, there are two very different courses available. One is to cultivate a small heart. It is the safest way to go, because it mini-mizes the sorrows. If our ambition is to avoid the troubles of life, the formula is simple: minimize entangling relation-ships and carefully avoid elevated and noble ideals and we will escape a host of problems. That is how to get through life easily.

But there is another path which Paul chose and which remains available to us, that is to open ourselves to others, to cultivate loving hearts. If you do that, you will enlarge your potential for pain, but also for impact on the lives of others.[3]

Paul chose the course that cultivated a large heart of love. He would have identified with these words: "Help can be bought. Care can be bought. Support can be bought. Loyalty of a sort can be bought. Sex can be bought. Some-times even forms of openness, tenderness, intimacy, and trust can be bought. Kindness can be bought. But—love is much more than the sum of its parts. Love cannot be bought."[4]

GIVING LOVE AWAY

In this text, Paul talks about how to give love away. He already illustrated part of the how in verse 7, with the picture of a mother who tenderly cares for her children. But that alone is an incomplete picture, because some people might conclude that a heart which gives love away can never be firm. And they slip into the quicksand mentality that believes love never confronts, never challenges, never corrects. To them, love is warm and syrupy, with no edges. Paul would disagree with that assessment; that is why, in the verses before us, he changes his illustration from a mother who cares to a father who instructs: "You are witnesses, and so is God, how devoutly and uprightly and blamelessly we behaved toward you believers; just as you know how we were exhorting and encouraging and imploring each one of you as a father would his own children" (1 Thessalonians 2:10-11).

It has been said that love without truth is hypocrisy and that truth without love is brutality. Paul could not have agreed more. His illustration of the mother stresses the tenderness of interaction with people. His illustration of the father stresses the more structured aspect of love. If Paul was gentle like a mother, he was also firm like a father. Paul's love was not simply sentimental. In verse 10 he pictures a father dealing with his children in instruction and discipline, as part of his love to them.

● As a father he exhibited love to them by being an example to them of *proper behavior*, which he defines with three words in verse 10. The first two words, *devoutly* and *uprightly*, go together. In unison, they stress the desire to live a life based on spiritual and biblical principles. The word translated "devoutly" refers to holiness. Now for some of us, holiness is a difficult concept to grasp. Dr. Gary Inrig tells of a time when he and his four-year-old son were traveling in the car and his boy introduced a statement with the words, "Holy cow!" Dr. Inrig took that opportunity to remind his little guy that their family didn't use that expression, and then tried to explain to him that only God and His things are holy. Stephen nodded his head in agreement, but added, "Dad, you can say holy Scriptures, can't you, 'cause the Bible's God's Word?" His father assured him he could, and on they drove with Dr. Inrig happily convinced that he had taught an important theological truth to his son. About ten minutes later there came an excited shout from little Stephen, *"Holy Scriptures, Dad — look over there!"*[5]

Sometimes it is difficult to put a finger on holiness. Perhaps Chuck Colson does the best job:

> There can be no holiness apart from the work of the Holy Spirit — in [stimulating] us through the conviction of sin and bringing us by grace to Christ, and in sanctifying us. Holiness is much more than a set of rules against sin. Holiness must be seen as the opposite of sin, [that is] conforming to the character of God — separating ourselves from sin and cleaving to Him is the essence of biblical holiness, and it is . . . a central theme running throughout Scripture.[6]

Holiness should impact us daily. It should prompt us to be very cautious with what we rent at the local video store. It should set off alarms when we think it is appropriate to lie to achieve our goals, or to deal under the table. A desire for holiness will pursue purity in dating relationships. It will scrutinize the lyrics of contemporary music. Holiness is repelled by other gods such as wealth. Holiness walks through the shopping centers of our minds and cleanses them. And holiness demonstrates love.

A believer in Jesus Christ is to live by a different ethical standard than that operative in the world—a standard inherent in the term *holiness.*

The second term Paul used to describe loving behavior is *uprightly. Upright* means "fair, honest," and relates to integrity of conduct. It refers to rightness of character and action, and is the same word translated in other places as "righteous." And uprightness *includes a value system,* an ethical compass grounded in spiritual realities. It rejects the relativism which claims there are no absolutes—a murky system of thought that pervades much of our culture. Mark Twain, although writing long ago, expresses the current mind-set: "Something moral is something you feel good after."

The flip side of that claims something immoral is something you feel bad after, which implies that you must try everything at least once; whatever produces a good result must be right, and whatever produces a bad result must be wrong. According to this distorted thinking process, actions or behavior patterns are not right or wrong in themselves, but only because of the results they produce.[7] How anemic! The underlying principle behind all of that is that love is not connected to absolutes or standards; love simply tolerates or welcomes all points of view.

Not so. Dr. Pierre Mornell, in his book, *Passive Men, Wild Women,* answers various questions about male and female relationships and roles in marriage. One question was about the failure of many fathers to be authority figures in the home. His answer: "I think in order to be a reasonable authority figure, *a man has to have values.* He has to believe in a set of "right" and "wrong" values and want to convey that set of values to his children."[8]

Allan Bloom, in his incredibly revealing text, *The Closing of the American Mind,* draws his breath and alerts us to something important: "The most important and most astonishing phenomenon of our time, all the more astonishing in being almost unnoticed: There is now an entirely new language of good and evil, originating in an attempt to get 'beyond good and evil,' and preventing us from talking with any conviction about good and evil anymore."⁹ And fathers, apparently, are among the worst offenders. It is no accident that Paul chooses the illustration of a father in these verses. Certainly mothers teach values, but the problem in so many homes today is that dads are silent in this area, either because they don't have sure standards or because, in some confused way, they think that their silence of toleration demonstrates love. It does not.

The existentialists and New Age philosophers argue that there is no standard of right or wrong. Everything depends. That kind of thinking derails on its own thesis — nothing is absolute except the absolute that nothing is absolute. That only produces confusion.

Paul says that as a demonstration of love, the Christian is to hunger after the righteous standards revealed in the Bible. The Word of God rules out sleek, self-satisfied, and halfhearted religion. Instead, it demands a consistent, burning desire to do what is right — to obey the Word of God.

Paul then adds a third description of loving behavior, with an example of something we all struggle with. The word *blameless* means that despite what the critic says about you, no real charges can be maintained. But what kind of behavior illustrates blamelessness? Certainly what we've already considered, but there is more. In Philippians 2:14-15, we read: "Do all things without grumbling or disputing, that you may prove yourselves to be blameless and innocent, children of God above reproach in the midst of a crooked and perverse generation, among whom you appear as lights in the world."

One distinguishing mark of a loving Christian is to be without blame in the area of grumbling or disputing. Now what is that saying to us? The word *grumbling* refers to expressing dissatisfaction, to muttering in a low voice. We would say, "complaining under our breath." And when we are constantly complaining about things and finding fault with others, it is extremely tough to convince people that we love them, and it is impossible to be found blameless.

But that's only half of it. Paul also mentions *disputing*, which means "skeptical questioning or criticism." It suggests thinking through a subject and reaching a contrary opinion, not to be helpful but just to be ornery. Richard Halverson cuts to the heart of the matter this way:

> Knowing what to do is easy . . . when you don't have to do it! One of the interesting and aggravating phenomena of our time is the vocal critic with all the answers. He always knows the way to go when he doesn't have to go himself. He's the expert pontificating on every conceivable issue. Free from having to follow through on a decision, he also feels free to make it for those who must bear the responsibility.
>
> What a difference between the players on the field and the spectator in the stands: The bleacher quarterback never makes a mistake!
>
> Of course, this isn't to say that dissent is wrong. Dissent is the stuff democracy is made of. But what about the dissenter's spirit? That's the thing. Let the spirit of the critic be sensitive to the burden of decision borne by the one criticized. "Do not judge, or you too will be judged. . . . Why do you look at the speck of sawdust in your brother's eye and pay no attention to the plank in your own eye?"[10]

The word *disputing* refers to the person who is always questioning and disagreeing with others. This person never has the joy of the Lord, and really does not want the label of "Love" pinned to his vest, because he is looking only for opportunities to disagree. There is a time, of course, for opposing opinions to be shared and discussed. But this verse is referring to the attitude of believers who constantly oppose.

Behavior that allows you to give your heart away, to truly demonstrate love, includes holiness, righteousness, and a lack of a complaining heart. And that only makes sense. You cannot show love to others when your heart is caustic and negative. And if you doubt the pervasiveness of complaining, just try to go the next twenty-four hours without doing it. Few of us are aware of how much we whine. Attempting such an exercise will bring some of us to our knees in humility. And it ought also to bring about some changes that will allow us to model, as Paul did, this characteristic of blamelessness.

• People who give their hearts away, who really love others, are not satisfied with permissive relationships. They are prepared to model holiness, righteousness, and blamelessness, even when it is painful. And it often is, especially if you move from a fatherly example in behavior, to a fatherly example in instruction in communication. Sometimes it is not enough to live an example; you also have to talk about it and challenge others in their spiritual lives. Paul did: "We were exhorting and encouraging and imploring" (1 Thessalonians 2:11).

A father can hope that his children will follow his example, but he also has the responsibility of teaching them how to live, and he does that in a spirit of love. The word *exhort* means "to criticize in love with a view toward a change." It assumes a problem, a weakness, a sin. It is saying, "I see a weakness and I correct it in love, so that you might be changed." It is not punishment; rather, it seeks a positive change in behavior. It pictures coming up to someone you know and throwing your arm over his shoulder and saying, "You know, I've noticed something recently, and I believe it would help you if. . . ." And then you kindly point out the problem and offer a solution. When you love others, you must be willing to do that. And if the correction comes to you, you need to be willing to respond positively, and not be bent out of shape.

Just how do *you* respond when a friend or close associate approaches you that way? Most of us are defensive, acting as if we have nothing to improve, as if we've arrived. *True love* not only points out weaknesses, but it also acknowledges weaknesses and prepares to deal with them positively. It could just be that the other person does have your best interests at heart.

What one weakness has been pointed out to you this past month? Did you blow your stack? Or, are you now working on it? And for those of you who enjoy dismantling others' lives through your criticism, when is the last time you approached that pastime with gentleness, with a sincere effort to help, not simply to brutalize? When you give your heart away, when you love others, that is the approach. Yet I am amazed at how many Christians are light years removed from it. They seem to feel that they have every right to pull out the heavy artillery and fire away. Why is that? They have cultivated small hearts, with no sensitivity gauges built in.

Exhorting also gives a gentle push. And once the person has begun to move in the direction of change, something else must occur . . . you must encourage them. The Williams' translation of this phrase says that "you cheer them on." In other words, as they make the effort to change, to improve in areas of weakness, to model holiness and attempt to reduce their tendency to gripe and complain, when that happens, you need to encourage them to keep it up. Encouraging words are messages of love.

> Our lives break down often, not so much because of the horrible things that happen to us, but because so few good things happen. Just a few of them along the way can be like branches we can cling to as we climb up a mountain trail. No matter how steep the climb, we can make it, if from time to time someone communicates to us that he or she loves us. . . ."[11]

Without realizing it, we fill important places in each other's lives. It's that way with a minister and congregation. Or with the guy at the corner grocery, the mechanic at the local garage, the family doctor, teachers, neighbors, co-workers. Good people, who are always "there," who can be relied upon in small, important ways. People who teach us, bless us, encourage us, support us, uplift us in the dailiness of life. We never tell them. I don't know why, but we don't.

And, of course, we fill that role ourselves. There are those who depend on us, watch us, learn from us, take from us. And we never know. Don't sell yourself short. You may never have proof of your importance, but you are more important than you think.

It reminds me of an old Sufi story of a good man who was granted one wish by God. The man said he would like to go about doing good without knowing about it. God granted his wish. And then God decided that it was such a good idea, he would grant that wish to all human beings. And so it has been to this day.[12]

But, sadly, sometimes exhorting—a gentle push and some encouraging—doesn't work. If people don't or won't change, the persons who wish to give their hearts away, to truly demonstrate love, must take another step.

Imploring is not a gentle word. It marches alongside courage with a tone of severity and an air of authority. It is not a gentle push or an arm on the shoulder; it's more like a kick in the pants. It is a word of conviction that is so necessary for those who love. To love someone is, ultimately, to confront them. Imploring must be firm and demonstrate conviction and backbone. To look the other way, to remain silent, does not demonstrate love.

Yet, under the banner of love, we are so afraid to call a spade a spade. No one wants to offend anyone. We are afraid to say that adultery is wrong. We are afraid to shout that homosexuality is an abomination to God and that abortion is murder. We are silent on the subject of premarital sex, when every day, on the average, three unmarried teenage girls will each have their third child. We hedge on confronting gossip and slander in the church. We do not have the nerve to stand and say, "This is wrong because the Word of God clearly says that it is wrong." Peter Marshall, former chaplain to the U.S. Senate, was not afraid to speak out about sin. When he preached people stood in line, crowded into the balconies of the church and filled the aisles to hear him. In a sermon on Elijah, where he described Elijah confronting the false religious leaders, Marshall ended his sermon with this statement: *"If God be God, then serve Him. If Baal be god, then serve him . . . and go to hell."* And then Marshall walked off the platform. Sometimes, when you love someone, you come to that.

LIVING WORTHY OF GOD

Why go to that length? Wouldn't it be far easier to simply ignore the problem and walk away? Just not rock the boat? Why bother? The reason is summarized in 1 Thessalonians 2:12: "So that you may walk in a manner worthy of the God who calls you into His own kingdom and glory."

For Paul there was a tight connection between Christian faith and life. Acceptance of the Gospel message carried with it the obligation to live a life consistent with that message. Paul was never content merely to gain large numbers of converts; he also pushed them to walk worthy of God. For a true believer the character of his daily life can never remain a matter of indifference, because of all that Christ has already done for him.

Having died for our sins, having offered Himself to God the Father as the One who took our penalty for sin, Christ has granted us forgiveness, if we accept His sacrifice by faith. If you have not done that, you must acknowledge your sin and Christ's sinlessness, your finiteness and Christ's infiniteness, your hopelessness and Christ's offer of hope. That is what Paul is driving at in verse 12 when he mentions our "being called to Christ's future kingdom." A day is coming when Jesus Christ will return to establish Himself as King. As believers we will then live with Him forever, and this is our hope, our motivation.

It is God's love for us — demonstrated in Christ — that pushes us to love others and to demonstrate that love in the way we behave and in the way we talk to them about difficult problems. God's everlasting love prompts our love, even when it's hard.

Ruth Harms Calkin, in her little book, *Lord, Don't You Love Me Anymore?* ties our hearts to God's love with these words:

He is seven years old
And he's my friend.
His eyes are merry, his hair is short
His nose is covered with freckles.
On a cold, rainy day we sat on the floor
Eating hot buttered popcorn.
The popcorn went down quickly.
But the questions came out slowly.

"If I told a lie today, would God stop loving me?"
  "No, of course not, David."
"What if I told two lies, or three
Would He stop loving me then?"
  "No, but you'd be unhappy in your heart."
"What if I punched Johnnie in the nose
And made his nose bleed—*hard?*
Would God stop loving me then?"
  "No, but you better not try it."
"What if I threw a rock and broke your window?
Would God stop loving me then?"
  "No, but you'd have to work hard to pay for it."
"What if I stepped on the snails
That ate all your flowers?
Would God stop loving me then?"
  "Not for a minute, David."

"When would God ever stop loving me?"
  "David, not until there is no more earth
  And no more heaven
  And no more love
  And no more God."
"Then it's never going to happen
No matter what."

"That's right, David.
Even if it sometimes *feels* like it might,
It's never going to happen,
No matter what."[13]

9
When It Is Even Harder to Love

*"See that you do not despise
one of these little ones, for I say to you,
that their angels in heaven continually behold
the face of My Father who is in heaven.
For the Son of Man has come to save
that which was lost.*

*"What do you think?
If any man has a hundred sheep,
and one of them has gone astray,
does he not leave the ninety-nine
on the mountains and go and search
for the one that is straying?
And if it turns out that he finds it,
truly I say to you, he rejoices over it
more than over the ninety-nine
which have not gone astray.
Thus it is not the will of your Father
who is in heaven that one of these
little ones perish.*

*"And if your brother sins, go and reprove
him in private; if he listens to you,
you have won your brother.
But if he does not listen to you,
take one or two more with you,
so that by the mouth of two or three witnesses
every fact may be confirmed.
And if he refuses to listen to them,
tell it to the church; and if he refuses to listen
even to the church, let him be to you
as a Gentile and a tax-gatherer.*

*" Truly I say to you, whatever you shall bind
on earth shall have been bound in heaven;
and whatever you loose on earth
shall have been loosed in heaven.*

*"Again I say to you, that if two of you agree
on earth about anything that they may ask,
it shall be done for them by My Father
who is in heaven. For where two or three
have gathered together in My name,
there I am in their midst."*

Matthew 18:10-20

I n his book *Strengthening Your Grip*, Chuck Swindoll
includes a letter that sets a backdrop for the subject
of this chapter. The letter reads:

During the past several years the Lord has been putting
me into a number of situations involving accountability
between Christians. I have and continue to struggle. And
I want to share what I am learning.

Two couples in my Sunday School class began living
with other partners before their eventual divorces. We
didn't know how to respond, especially to the one woman
who brought her boyfriend to class. So we ignored them.
Just great, huh?

Some time later two classmates started living with fel-
lows. And that stirred up lots of things for me. About the
same time a friend dropped by on a business trip and
discussed a current case with a rather well-known pastor
in his locale who was sleeping around. At a Christian
college, coeds came for help with sexual involvements
with married employees.

Talk about a thickening plot! In response, I have been
grappling with biblical and psychological concepts of relationship, confrontation, accountability, etc. Here are
some of my observations to date:

In a total of nineteen years I have neither experienced

nor heard of any community-level confrontation. It is as though the progressive confrontation of Matthew 18:15 were not in Scripture. I cannot help but conclude that the trend among Christians to divorce, sin sexually, etc., will increase unless Scripture is taken seriously in the church in this area of confrontation.

I believe that if our relationships in the church are not sufficiently developed such that others can see and respond to trouble brewing in our marriages (or our lives), then we are in big trouble. Who will help us?[1]

The answer to that question? You and I are to help. If the record of Scripture, and specifically Matthew 18, is taken seriously, then we as believers are instructed to care enough for fellow believers that we will *confront* them where there is continual personal sin in their lives. Now that is not easy, nor is it without pain, but it is part of love.

The delight of being close to someone is always accompanied by the peril of hurting or being hurt by that someone. Intimacy and the potential for pain go hand in hand. You cannot have one without the other. [Yet] a sociologist studying the average Christian church would see no essential difference in the quality of its human relationships and those of some local club, say a community service group or a country club.[2]

Now, before we explore this any further, I'd like to make an important clarification. In the minds of some people, *confronting* seems incompatible with loving each other and not judging others. Let me show you that apparent contradiction from two verses in Matthew, "And if your brother sins, go and reprove him in private; if he listens to you, you have won your brother" (18:15). "Do not judge lest you be judged yourselves" (7:1). How is it possible to confront someone with their sin and yet not judge that one?

It is possible because of the difference between judging and confronting. In Matthew 7, Jesus is saying, in essence: "Don't be judgmental. Do not adopt a critical attitude, a condemning spirit." The verb *judge* was used primarily about the negative, caustic judgments we make of other people.

Judging is a hasty response, often emotional in nature and frequently wrong. It is a verdict given *without all the facts,* based on only superficial findings or hearsay. We are also guilty of judging when we reach hasty, premature, and prejudicial conclusions regarding someone's heart and motives.

Confrontation, on the other hand, is a slow response. It can be emotional, but it is controlled. Also, it has the distinct advantage of having gathered all available facts. Jesus makes that clear in Matthew 18:16: "But if he does not listen to you, take one or two more with you, so that by the mouth of two or three witnesses every fact may be confirmed."

The word *confirmed* means "to be established as true, to be validated." Biblical confrontation deals in the arena of truth, not gossip. And the intent of confrontation is not condemnation but restoration.

THE TONE OF CONFRONTATION

Given that clarification, confrontation becomes a proper and biblical approach. However, before we go bursting into people's lives with all guns firing, we need to consider seriously the *tone of confrontation* established in Matthew 18. That tone begins long before we go head to head with someone. Look at verses 8 and 9 of Matthew 18 to see the attitude we must cultivate in our lives: "If your hand or your foot causes you to stumble, cut it off and throw it from you; it is better for you to enter life crippled or lame, than having two hands or two feet, to be cast into the eternal fire. And if your eye causes you to stumble, pluck it out and throw it from you. It is better for you to enter life with one eye, than having two eyes, to be cast into the hell of fire."

Jesus assumes that the individual who personally con-

fronts someone will do so with true humility, *having carefully examined his or her own life.* Jesus is not advocating a
physical self-maiming, but a personal, moral examination.
The bottom line means this: *Take drastic action in dealing
with whatever tempts you to sin.*

Tearing out the eye means then, "Don't look." Behave as
if you had actually torn out your eye and could not see the
objects that previously caused you to sin. Cutting off your
hand or foot means that you behave as if you had actually
cut off your hands and feet and were now crippled and
could not do the things which previously caused you to sin.

Dealing with others confrontationally then, begins with a
serious examination of your own life and a confrontation of
sin there. But there is another aspect that occurs *during* the
confrontation and really cements the purpose of it in your
mind. Jesus introduces this element in Matthew 18:12-14:
"What do you think? If a man has a hundred sheep and one
of them has gone astray, does he not leave the ninety-nine
on the mountains and go and search for the one that is
straying? And if it turns out that he finds it, truly I say to
you, he rejoices over it more than over the ninety-nine
which have not gone astray. Thus it is not the will of your
Father who is in heaven that one of these little ones
perish."

In the Palestine of the first century, it was easy for sheep
to wander and go astray. The pastureland was in the hill
country and there were few restraining walls or fences
around the pastures. At best, the grass was sparse. As a
result, the sheep frequently disappeared. But the Palestin-
ian shepherds were experts at tracking them down and
would follow them for miles. The shepherds made the most
strenuous and sacrificial efforts to find a lost sheep.

As we consider confrontation, we must remember that
God cares for people individually; we should reflect that
individual care and love in our confrontation of a Christian
who is wandering. The Parable of the Sheep illustrates the
forgiving love of God which seeks to reclaim sinners. God

cares for believers as a shepherd cares for his sheep. If one of them is lost, He makes every effort to recover it and is ecstatic if He succeeds. The way God deals with His wandering sheep is the way we are to deal with those we confront in love.

The exercise described by Matthew is a rescue operation, designed not so much to condemn but to bring us "heart to heart." You'll notice that verse 15 tells us that the goal of confrontation is "to win" the other person. The reconciling process breaks through the icy wall of alienation into the warm embrace of renewed fellowship. The purpose in all of this is not to score points, but to win the person back. In other words, you regain him as a friend, if his sin has separated the two of you. Or, you save her from further negative consequences of her actions, by helping her face it and deal with it.

The goal during confrontation is rescue. And at such moments, we must take a deep breath and remind ourselves that we serve a God with an odd penchant for bunglers and wanderers. It does us good occasionally to remember parts of His track record. He called a man named Abram to a great destiny, but he promptly ran off to Egypt, then dreamed up a scam to protect himself, and landed his wife in Pharaoh's harem. Then, he was evicted from the country. Still, he is identified as "the friend of God."

And God is the type to pick up a murderer named Moses, who in one angry moment torpedoed his career as the next Pharaoh, and yet still used him to rescue His people from Egypt. The trail continues through David's mid-life affair, to Simon Peter, whose apostleship reminds us that God has a future for people who blurt out things they don't mean. We must never lose sight of such examples in the process of confrontational love, and always remember that restoration is the goal.[3]

The great artist Herkomer was born in the Black Forest of Europe. His father was a simple woodcutter. When the artist rose to fame in London and built his studio there, he invited his very elderly father to spend the rest of his life with him. And so he came to London. He was very fond of molding clay and all day he made things, but as the years passed, his hands began to lose their ability. He often went upstairs at night with a sad heart—the heart of an old man who believed his best days were gone. His son's quick eyes of love detected that, and when his father was asleep he would slip downstairs and take in hand the pieces of clay which his dad had left—with their evidences of defect and failure—and with his own wonderful touch, he would make them as beautiful as they could be made. When his old father came down in the morning, and took up the work he had left the night before, he would hold it up to the light, rub his hands and say, "I can do it as well as I ever did."

God takes *our* failures and remolds them. He looks for the wandering sheep and restores them. And that is the tone that must accompany the process of confrontation.

THE PERSON CONFRONTED

As we look again at verse 15, we see *the person involved,* the fellow Christian who is sinning! This sin is of such a nature that it cannot be winked at. Jesus has in mind a continual pattern of sin. Now the Lord does not tell us what the sin is. We have to determine that from clear statements in other parts of the Word of God. Let me suggest two such passages: Galatians 5:19-21 and 1 Corinthians 5:11:

"Now the deeds of the flesh are evident, which are: immorality, impurity, sensuality, idolatry, sorcery, enmities, strife, jealousy, outbursts of anger, disputes, dissensions, factions, envyings, drunkenness, carousings, and things like these, of which I forewarn you just as I have forewarned you that those who practice such things shall not inherit the kingdom of God."

"I wrote to you not to associate with any so-called brother if he should be an immoral person, or covetous, or an idolater, or a reviler, or a drunkard, or a swindler — not even to eat with such a one."

If such activities are practiced, loving confrontation with the person is required. Now I am not suggesting a harsh, uncompassionate assault on all who *temporarily* lapse into sin and soon after that acknowledge and repent of the wrong. No, this involves much more than that. This is a clear case of continual, sinful activity that is taking its toll on the person, as well as on others in the church, whether or not that sin is specifically directed their way. Anne Ortlund has such a good word to say here: "We know plenty about each others' failures, but we know almost nothing about 'tough love.' Christian fellowship must not only be supportive, [it must be] corrective. To plant a garden but never weed it will produce a garden that is a mess. To fellowship in a group of believers without accountability and correctiveness will eventually produce a group of believers who are a mess."[4]

When prolonged personal sin is discovered in the life of another believer in the church, then we must deal with it. I know that sounds difficult, but please keep in mind that *the cost of avoiding or repressing the conflict is usually greater than the cost of facing and dealing with the conflict.* The lingering agony of the unresolved concern, the energy sapped in bottling up feelings or denying needs, and the clever games that must be played in order to avoid the confrontation, are rarely worth the short-term pain of dealing with the problem.

Since that is true, we need to think through how the actual confrontation should occur. When you are aware of continuous personal sin in the life of a believer, what are the steps in the encounter of confrontation you need to take?

• The first part of verse 15 starts us in the right direction: "If your brother sins, go and reprove him in private; if he listens to you, you have won your brother." The verb *go* is a command that is singular in person. It means that we *as individuals* have a responsibility in this area. But so often we rationalize and excuse ourselves from this action. We think "I don't want to get involved, it's really none of my business," or, "Just what constitutes sin, anyway? Besides, I'm not trained or experienced in something like this, and I really should pray about it for a while" (usually a long while). We may even catch ourselves choking on expressions such as, "Look, it's probably just a passing thing and it will go away by itself; after all, I could be mistaken."

All of those statements may have some element of truth to them, but they do not relieve us of our responsibility. In fact, if we are honest, we really don't have a problem in this verse with the word *sin;* our problem is with the word *go.* But the moment I say, "Hey, this is not my responsibility," I have turned the church into a religious club, at best.

There is, however, a word of caution here. When you go, you should go slowly. You must first attempt to gather all the facts. But you still must go. Whether you make one visit or more is not stated. That may depend on the situation, but still, you must go.

And having done so, the text indicates you must go in private. This action of love is between you and the other person. Nobody else. Your responsibility is to go to the person, not to a committee, not to a prayer or Bible study group, not to a pastor, or another close friend. To go to any or all of those individuals or groups first is to violate a heart of love. You see, Christ's method avoids the risk of gossip, because you begin by going to the source of the problem.

John Dryden, a seventeenth-century British poet, once commented on our tendency to gossip:

> There is a lust in man no charm can tame,
> of loudly publishing his neighbor's shame.
> Hence, on eagles' wings immortal scandals fly,
> while virtuous actions are but born and die.

Dietrich Bonhoeffer was correct when he observed, "When the tongue is under our authority, much that is unnecessary remains unsaid. But the helpful and essential thing can be said in a few words."

• But you'll note Jesus' further instruction; having gone in private, you are to *reprove* that person. This word means that you expose the sin to the person so as to bring conviction. It assumes that there is a serious problem, a continuing sin, and it says, "I see a weakness, a sin, and I am here to point it out to you in love so that you may be changed." Your business then is to bring the person to see that they have indeed sinned. Your desire is to seek a positive change in their behavior. So, as directly but as kindly as you know how, you explain your concerns, describe the problem as you see it, and then ask for a response. The initial confrontation is simply putting your cards on the table and allowing that person to respond. Remember, in doing this you must be honest and upfront, but you must deal with truth. Don't exaggerate for effect. Be brief and to the point.

Recently, I read with fascination an article on the subject of biblical confrontation. The author made these wise observations about rebuking:

> Rebuke, therefore, emerges as part of the responsibility that Christians in a marriage and in a church owe to one another. It is the duty of love. Yet, often in the guise of love, we keep silent. One of the surest tests of friendship is whether or not we will tell a friend about his faults. As friends, however, we believe we love too much to interfere in the life of fellow Christians. Yet, it may not be love that keeps us silent. It may be indifference. We may draw back, not because we care too much but because we care too little. If we refuse to confront, we can make no moral difference in another person's life.
>
> Rebuke should be neither the first word in a relationship nor the only word nor the major word. Yet, at times, it is a necessary word. By the grace of God and through the confrontation of those who care about us we can be better than we are.[5]

• Having gone and having laid the issue out, the ball now shifts to the other person's court. It is now their responsibility to react, and Christ indicates in verse 15 that the best response is that he *listens* to you. The word means "to admit wrongdoing and be reconciled to the person."

In your experience, can you remember a confrontation having that kind of response? The fact that we can only rarely draw from our memory banks a limited number of those kinds of responses indicates the tragedy in so many Christians' lives. A well-known Jewish rabbi of our own day commented sadly, "I wonder whether there is any one in these times who accepts reproof."

Or, if someone has confronted you, do you listen, or do you become defensive? Do you try desperately to protect yourself against the assignment of fault? Do you lash out at those who confront you? Some people are prepared to sacrifice everyone else to preserve their self-image of perfection. Others, rather than listening, will bad-mouth the person who confronts, claiming that they have been wronged, attacked, and hurt. Rather than listening, they may seek for a "more loving and understanding" church.

Martin Luther observed, "The ultimate proof of the sinner is that he does not know his own sin." My friends, as long as we insist on blaming others for our actions, our sins, we will remain victims.

You can pick up a newspaper any day and find a story about an automobile accident involving teenagers. You will probably read that the driver was going too fast, lost control, and crossed the line. More than likely, the teenager was drunk. But when people talk to his friends they will swear, "Sure, he had a few drinks—but he wasn't drunk! If he was drunk, why, he wouldn't have driven."

Then you discover from blood tests that the others who were killed in the accident were also drinking heavily. You wonder what got into them. Intelligent, all-American young people. But you realize, *No matter what they had heard about driving drunk, each believed, "I am the exception."*[6]

That is how people feel when confronted with a sin: "Look, you don't understand, this is different."

• What follows in the verses before us does not have to take place if the individual listens. If he does, that's the end of the matter. It has remained between you and the other person and it is settled. He has been challenged, convicted, and is going to change. But, if he will not listen, verse 16 takes us another step: "But if he does not listen to you, take one or two more with you, so that by the mouth of two or three witnesses every fact may be confirmed."

You then take one or two trusted people back with you to this person to repeat the process in exactly the same manner. The wisdom here is clear. The people who accompany you will perhaps be able to help convince the person of error. At the very least, they will be witnesses to the process, to your words, so that nothing becomes distorted. They will be able to affirm that you made efforts to properly deal with the situation, and will see and hear how the offending person responds. If the person softens, admits the sin and deals with it, that is the end of the matter, with as few as three people involved.

Unfortunately, that is not often how it goes, since the person usually becomes more adamant. Look at verse 17: "And if he refuses to listen to them, tell it to the church; and if he refuses to listen even to the church, let him be to you as a Gentile and a tax-gatherer." The phrase *refuses to listen* is stronger than the similar words of verse 16. It is more than a lack of positive response, but quite literally suggests "paying absolutely no attention to your counsel." There is no sign of sorrow, of repentance, of a desire to change.

At that point, the sinful actions can no longer be considered privileged information. The *church* here refers to the locally organized group of believers; the information must be shared with the body at large. The hope is that when this happens, the person will repent and will change. This is why, in our church, we read the names of individuals who are excluded at Communion. It must be told.

If they do not listen then, the Lord says they are to

become to the congregation and each individual within it as "a Gentile and a tax-gatherer." That means that you are not to have fellowship or association with that person. Dr. Paul Benware, a professor at Moody Bible Institute, makes this action very clear when he writes:

> If the individual refuses to repent, the church is to with-hold fellowship. In such a situation, believers are to have no fellowship with him/her—no conversations, no dinner invitations, no social get-togethers, no joint prayer with her—until repentance takes place. If this action does not bring repentance and he/she persists in sin, the last step is excommunication. The offender is formally removed from the membership or fellowship life of the church. Because the local church is part of the greater, universal church, other local [churches] should respect and support a church's actions of discipline. It does no good if anoth-er local church gladly receives an unrepentant individual under discipline as a new member.[7]

In our twentieth-century mentality this sounds so out of place. We are so laid back, so tolerant, that these actions invoke images of witch hunts and crusades. It is not like that at all. G. Campbell Morgan, a godly and gifted commu-nicator of God's Word in this country and England, wrote powerfully to this point:

> The theme is difficult. I can talk freely here. I am under my own vine and fig tree. I hate discipline! I would rather do anything than go and tell a man about his fault. I would rather do anything than have to tell a man he has done something wrong. I always feel I am the culprit. But evil must not be tolerated within the fellowship of the Christian Church. You have no business, if there is someone over there with whom you are not on speaking terms, to remain inside the Church. Out with you, and get it settled! You are paralyzing the fellowship. Evil must not be tolerated; wrong conduct must be judged; the tolerated evil is leaven-ing the whole camp and corrupting the Church of God.
> To allow a wrongdoer to continue in Church member-

ship is to inflict wrong on him by giving him a false sense of security. Put him out, in order that he may see the darkness, and that the lurid light of judgment may arrest him. Let him know there is no shelter for a man who persistently sins. Do not lull him into false security by allowing him to stay in the fellowship, and imagine that he may continue in sin that grace may abound. The Church must be pure. No consideration of delicacy, of sensitiveness, of peace, must prevent our loyalty to Christ. . . .

And let it never be forgotten that repentance is always a door to reinstatement. Let us have no lengthy probation for a sinning brother. Get him in. The Church is not the abode of absolutely perfect men and women! The Church is a nursery; the Church is a home.[8]

THE AUTHORITY FOR CHURCH DISCIPLINE

Now someone might still say, "But what gives us the *authority* to take such steps?" That authority is given to the church by Jesus Christ Himself, in Matthew 18:18-20: "Truly I say to you, whatever you shall bind on earth shall have been bound in heaven; and whatever you loose on earth shall have been loosed in heaven. Again I say to you, that if two of you agree on earth about anything that they may ask, it shall be done for them by My Father who is in heaven. For where two or three have gathered together in My name, there I am in their midst."

Christ is saying that if the procedure of loving confrontation is followed as He outlined it, then when someone is removed from the membership by the church, that binding decision is ratified in heaven; that is, it is sanctioned by God. Conversely, whoever is allowed back into the membership upon repentance — whoever is "loosed" as the text says — that same decision on earth is approved by God. That is why the two or three people are mentioned here and in verse 16. It is not easy for them to pursue confrontation. But if they follow the guidelines here, Jesus Christ is saying to them, "I am with you in this." The church and her leadership have God's authority to decide on matters of discipline, and the decisions of the church regarding what is or is not appropriate in its membership must be regarded as final.

There are two reasons for church discipline. One is for the sake of the erring person; his Christian friends care enough to help him to a place of correction and accountability and to restore him to God and to the church. The second reason is the integrity of the church and its witness.

The question of church discipline was a basic issue during the Protestant Reformation. And as far back as 1525 the Anabaptists had made this an issue. Much later, John Calvin added to the life of the Reformed Church the doctrine of church discipline. Through the centuries, this concern has been a part of great spiritual movements such as the Weslyan Revival, the East African revival, and the Keswick Movement. And it remains an essential for the people of God today. In fact, we can say that where there is no discipline, there is no true church.

If people would only listen to rebuke, would respond with sorrow and repentance, the extremes of discipline would not be necessary. And yet, the tragedy is that people think they can go on sinning with no negative consequences. This is not true. Sin will ultimately provide its own consequences, even if no one confronts. I think this is the saddest part of all of this. It isn't the Lord who loses. It isn't even the church who loses. The sinner loses! I have never seen a genuinely joyful Christian who is sinning habitually and blatantly. Never! And I have never met one who is living in sin who could look me straight in the eye and say, "These are the happiest years of my life."

The Danish philosopher Soren Kierkegaard is often very difficult to read. But in his parable of the wild duck, there is a splendid illustration of how the soul declines from its ideals. This duck was flying in the springtime northward across Europe. During the flight he came down in a Danish barnyard where there were tame ducks and he enjoyed some of their corn. He stayed for an hour, then for a day, then for a week, then for a month. Finally, because he relished the good fare and safety of the barnyard, he stayed all summer. One autumn day when a flock of wild ducks were wending their way southward again, they passed over the barnyard, and the duck heard their cries. He was stirred with a strange thrill of joy and delight, and with a great flapping of wings he rose in the air to join his old comrades in their flight.

But he found that his good fare had made him so soft and heavy that he could rise no higher than the eaves of the barn. So he dropped back again to the barnyard and said to himself, "Oh well, my life is safe here and the food is good." Every spring and autumn when he heard the wild ducks honking, his eyes would gleam for a moment and he would begin to flap his wings. But finally the day came when the wild ducks flew over him and uttered their cry, but he paid not the slightest attention to them.[9]

If God is calling you, then by all means, respond now, while you can still hear His voice.

10
LOVE'S DOUBLE REVERSE

*Bless those who persecute you; bless
and curse not. Rejoice with those who rejoice,
and weep with those who weep.
Be of the same mind toward one another;
do not be haughty in mind, but associate
with the lowly. Do not be wise
in your own estimation.*

*Never pay back evil for evil to anyone.
Respect what is right in the sight of all men.
If possible, so far as it depends on you,
be at peace with all men.*

*Never take your own revenge, beloved,
but leave room for the wrath of God,
for it is written, "Vengeance is Mine,
I will repay," says the Lord.*

*"But if your enemy is hungry,
feed him, and if he is thirsty, give him a drink;
for in so doing you will heap burning coals
upon his head."*

*Do not be overcome by evil,
but overcome evil with good.*

Romans 12:14-21

In Judith Viorst's children's book, *I'll Fix Anthony*, the younger brother complains about the way his older brother, Anthony, treats him:

My brother Anthony can read books now, but he won't read any books to me. He plays checkers with Bruce from his school. But when I want to play he says, "Go away or I'll clobber you." I let him wear my Snoopy sweatshirt, but he never lets me borrow his sword. Mother says deep down in his heart Anthony loves me. Anthony says deep down in his heart he thinks I stink. Mother says deep, deep down in his heart, where he doesn't even know it, Anthony loves me. Anthony says deep, deep down in his heart he still thinks I stink. When I'm six I'll fix Anthony. . . .

When I'm six I'll float, but Anthony will sink to the bottom. I'll dive off the board, but Anthony will change his mind. I'll breathe in and out when I should, but Anthony will only go glug, glug. When I'm six my teeth will fall out, and I'll put them under the bed, and the tooth fairy will take them away and leave dimes. Anthony's teeth won't fall out. He'll wiggle and wiggle them, but they won't fall out. I might sell him one of my teeth, but I might not. . . .

> Anthony is chasing me out of the playroom. He says I stink. He says he is going to clobber me. I have to run now, but I won't have to run when I'm six. When I'm six, I'll fix Anthony.[1]

Most of us know the feeling, don't we? And it is a feeling that screams at you when someone deliberately hurts you. When they methodically and meticulously set out to harm you, when it seems that they are doing everything they can to make your life miserable, the sirens begin to whine. It is so natural to want to fight back, to rally your forces and charge ahead, to lash back and exact your pound of flesh, to get revenge.

> People bury hatchets but carefully tuck away the map which tells where their hidden weapon lies. We put our resentments in cold storage and then pull the switch to let them thaw out again. Our grudges are taken out to the lake to drown them . . . and we end up giving them a swimming lesson. How often have we torn up the canceled note, but hung on to the wastebasket that holds the pieces?[2]

Too many times, more than we care to remember, we have kept track of our grudges. And sometimes, we frankly enjoy our revenge or say we do. At other times, it eats the lining of our stomach and keeps us running out of Tums. One way or the other, the desire for revenge is something we all deal with.

As Dr. Theodore Rubin dissects the subject of love, he lists its enemies. On his list, Enemy 18 is rejection and vengeance:

> Rejection and vengeance go hand in hand. Arbitrary rejection is often a form of vindictive vengeance and the infliction of cruelty. Regardless of form, vindictiveness and rejection are the basis of antagonistic relating. This is the antithesis of love and is invariably corrosive to all concerned. The antidote is forgiveness—which is only possible with love.[3]

THE PRINCIPLE OF BLESSING

In the city of Corinth in Greece, a city in which he endured terrific pain from Christians, Paul wrote the New Testament letter to the Romans. And toward the end of that letter, he worked through some thoughts on relationships. He reviewed in his mind his own journey, his own pain, his own suffering at the hands of people, and then he drew some conclusions about how to deal with all of that. He couched it under the banner of love, because without love what he suggests as a general principle staggers the imagination. "Bless those who persecute you; bless and curse not" (Romans 12:14).

A person who "persecutes" you has it in for you, is constantly watching you, waiting for you to foul up, so that they can expose you, embarrass you, or torture you. The persecution Paul is thinking about could take a variety of forms, running the gamut from verbal abuse and social alienation to physical violence. It is frequently unjust and malicious treatment directed your way, perhaps provoked by your good behavior. Sometimes it happens because of what you believe as a Christian. Its artillery can be aimed at you from the guns of non-Christians or from Christians, right within the church.

So what do you do? What's the principle Paul wants to galvanize into your heart? The verb *bless* means "to ask for God's blessing on someone." Believe it or not, you are to actively seek this person's good and pray for God's blessing in their life. Some suggest that means praying for their forgiveness.

Now that certainly isn't what *we* would have recommended as a general principle. We might have suggested rallying our forces, lobbying for our point of view, or strategizing about our counterattack. Right? But when did we entertain the idea of praying for the person who knocked us down, pushed us around, ignored our advice, or hurt us deeply?

That's where we start, and that's the easy part, because the word *bless* also means "to speak well of someone." It's the opposite of cursing. To *curse* somebody means "to ask God to withhold His grace from their life" or "to actually inflict pain on that person." We're not to slip into that game, but instead are to speak well of them. That means that we do not go around bad-mouthing people who are not nice to us. We don't run them down or speak harshly about them to others. Instead, we speak well of them. We find something that we can approve and say so to other people when we speak of that person.

THE ATTITUDE OF BLESSING

Because this is so difficult, we need to constantly remind ourselves of what love is. Love is the *will* to extend yourself for the purpose of nurturing your own or another person's spiritual growth. Genuine love is volitional rather than emotional. The person who truly loves does so because of a decision, a commitment to be loving, whether or not the feeling of love is present. Now if that feeling is there, so much the better; but if not, the commitment and will to love are still expressed.

• We need to constantly rehearse and review this commitment if we hope to model the attitude of blessing beginning in Romans 12:15: "Rejoice with those who rejoice, and weep with those who weep."

Someone has said, "If we could read the secret history of our enemies, we should find in each man's life sorrow and suffering enough to disarm all hostility." People who make a career of pushing others around, who seem to enjoy inflicting misery, often operate out of an arena of personal pain. And behind the austere, cold, calculating mask, their hidden tears cause their makeup to run, their eyes to swell, and their throat to tighten. And part of the attitude of blessing your enemies is to identify with them in their sorrows, their pain. *Weeping* means "sorrow, pain, and grief of heart." But if we quit loving the moment it becomes difficult, we never really discover compassion, because *compassion* is *"your* pain in *my* heart."

Normally, we don't think along these lines when the enemy's artillery is hitting its target — us. At that moment we are concerned with *our* pain and our ability to go on. While that's appropriate, we often miss the opportunity to identify with our enemies in *their* pain and sorrow, to reach out to them when their world is collapsing, when their heart is breaking. That is the attitude of blessing.

All of us carry luggage filled with pain. Sometimes that pain is physical, but more often it is hidden emotional scars. And every once in a while, we need someone to lean our way with comfort and ease the load. And that is where Paul indicates we come in.

> Let me come in where you are weeping, friend,
>   and let me take your hand.
> I, who have known a sorrow such as yours,
>   can understand.
> Let me come in — I would be very still
>   beside you in your grief.
> I would not bid you cease your weeping, friend;
>   tears bring relief.
> Let me come in — I would only breathe a prayer,
>   and hold your hand.
> For I have known a sorrow such as yours,
>   and understand.[5]

You'll notice also that even before Paul hints of comfort, he introduces rejoicing, because that is more difficult. When someone has shrapneled you with grief, unjust criticism, and pain, and then that same person succeeds, or has something positive occur in his life that should have been in yours, it is tough to congratulate him, isn't it? To sincerely say, "I'm happy for you"? But love does that.

● But there's more. Look at verse 16: "Be of the same mind toward one another; do not be haughty in mind, but

associate with the lowly. Do not be wise in your own estimation." To "be of the same mind" suggests a movement
toward unity, an ability to live in harmony even if you
disagree with someone. Paul is not advocating a uniformity
of thought and behavior; rather, he is talking about an ability to get along with each other. Sometimes we reject sug-
gestions out of hand simply because the people making
them have given us problems in the past. We've had a
conflict and so we write them off, even though their subse-
quent ideas may be valuable. Love agrees to disagree at
times and not to treat prejudicially those who have hurt us.
Being of the same mind means that we treat people with
nonpreferential, nonpartisan love.

And Paul handcuffs to that a clear warning regarding
pride. When you are being hounded by somebody who just
won't let up, who is constantly after you, it is very natural
to become defensive and even condescending when you
talk to or about them. You have a natural inclination to
despise them, to look down on them because they have hurt
you. And in order to protect yourself, you build yourself up
and begin to think high thoughts about yourself. All the
time you put them further down and become more convinced that you are right and they are wrong. You become
unmovable. And instead of bridging the gap between the
two of you, you let it widen until it becomes an uncrossable
chasm. When that occurs, you are guilty of preferential
treatment. You treat those who don't hurt you one way, and
those who do in a very different way. Biblical love reverses
that flow by not being preferential in its treatment of
others.

THE ACTIONS THAT BLESS

You may say, "Look, that's great . . . but how do I really
behave that way?" You do it by modeling the actions of
blessing that Paul adds in the balance of our text.

• We are to be *nonvindictive.* "Never pay back evil for evil to anyone. . . . Never take your own revenge, beloved, but leave room for the wrath of God, for it is written, 'Vengeance is Mine, I will repay,' says the Lord" (Romans 12:17, 19).

The word *evil* means "wrong or harm inflicted on you by another person's malicious intent." In other words, the hurt you feel didn't just happen; it wasn't simply an unfortunate set of circumstances, but was a planned attack. When such actions invade your airspace, Paul cautions you not to get even, not to be vindictive or retaliate.

We all tilt that way, don't we? We're like the elderly lady who was driving a big, expensive new car and was preparing to back into a parallel parking space, when suddenly a young man in a small sports car zoomed into her space ahead of her. The lady angrily asked why he had done that, when he could tell she was trying to park there. His response was simply, "Because I'm young and I'm quick." The young man then entered a store. When he came back out a few minutes later, he found the lady using her big, new car as a battering ram—backing up and then running into his car. He angrily demanded an explanation. Her response was, *"Because I'm old and I'm rich!"*

There's a lot of that lady in all of us—we all have an inclination to punish others. We feel that if we treat them in the way they have treated us, we are only giving them what they deserve. The woman's revengeful style basically said that she felt hurt by life and, therefore, she had a right to strike back. But the inevitable result of trying to get even is that we increase the conflict and alienation, and our own resentment and bitterness build. Leo Buscaglia, in his fine book, *Loving Each Other,* is to the point:

> When we feel wronged, we feel we have a right, therefore to demand justice. We believe that justice has been accomplished only when we can hurt those who have hurt us, disappoint those who have disillusioned us, make suffer those who have injured us and given us pain.

They must experience our revenge at once and preferably continue to experience it forever. We are certain that
wrong will be righted only in this way. Only then will
the slate be wiped clean and our pain disappear. After
all, we rationalize, it was the other's fault. Why then
should we be the one to suffer? We seek vengeance for
we know that the experience will be sweet. But do we
find it so? How many of us have gone to great pains to
avenge a wrongdoing, only to find that once we have had
our revenge, we have accomplished little more than finding ourselves loveless and alone? What satisfaction is
there in causing another to suffer if our pain still remains? What is the use of demanding an eye for an
eye — when having plucked out the other's eye, we still
have only one eye?[6]

Revenge never satisfies, and it makes love impossible.
That's why Paul counsels us to trust God to take care of the
situation. God will not bungle; He will not be too lenient or
too severe; He will ultimately do what is best.

• And if we can believe that, the second action Paul
prescribes can become part of our experience: "Respect
what is right in the sight of all men" (v. 17).

The verb *respect* means literally "to think ahead of time."
As believers we are to think before we respond; we are to
consider the correct action, the right response, before we
lash out impulsively. Let's look at how other versions of the
Bible render this verse:

"See that your *public behavior* is above criticism."

"Aim to live *above reproach* in the sight of every one."

"Do things in such a way that everyone can see you are
honest clear through."

"Determine on the noblest ways in dealing with all
people."

Paul is calling Christians to live out the implications of
the Gospel. Our lives are to be on such a high plane that
even nonbelievers will recognize their quality. Put another
way, as Christians we are to live consistently — even in the

face of agony and persecution—so much so that our enemies, those who are intent on making us look bad or feel pain, will not have a legitimate reason to attack us.

The reformer John Calvin said, "What is meant is that we ought diligently to labor, in order that all may be edified by our honest dealings . . . that they may, in a word, perceive the good, and the sweet odor of our life, by which they must be attracted to the LOVE of God."[7]

It is our consistency that will disarm our enemies. It is our balanced, sane response to the inequities and cruelties from those who hound us that carries the greatest influence. In light of this, the question that swirls most often in my mind is, "How consistent am I?" Chuck Swindoll describes consistency this way:

> It is a living model of patience, determination, and strength—regardless of shifty, rootless times. The blasts of ridicule and criticism may punch it in the face—but consistency stands and takes it as silently as a bronze statue takes the tempest. One poet calls it "a jewel," another "an anchor of iron." It knows little of ups and downs, highs or lows, blue Mondays or holiday hangovers. It's an obvious mark of maturity. It's hanging in there day in and day out, in spite of everything that could get you sidetracked.
>
> Consistency, it's the jewel worth wearing,
>   it's the anchor worth weighing
>   it's the thread worth weaving
>   it's the battle worth winning.[8]

● And when we win the battle of consistency, we tend to be *harmonious* in our relationships with others—even our enemies. "If possible, so far as it depends on you, be at peace with all men" (v. 18).

The word *peace* has as its root meaning "to reconcile." It suggests bringing people together, not driving them apart. It pictures building bridges, not burning them behind you. It begs for grace and it recoils from law. It thrives on compassion; it withers under criticism.

Do you work for peace? Or do you find some inner satisfaction in having others upset with you? I know people who go out of their way to accumulate enemies. They remind me of the knight who returned to the castle at twilight in a state of total disarray—dented armor, helmet falling off, face bloody, horse crippled, and the knight himself about to fall off his limping horse. "What hath befallen you, Sir Knight?" asked the lord of the castle. "O Sire," answered the knight, "I have been laboring in your service, robbing and plundering and pillaging *your enemies* in the West." "You what?" cried the lord. "I don't have any enemies in the West." "Oh," said the knight, *"you do now!"*

You've met people who enjoy accumulating enemies. They relish a good fight, whether at home, work, or in church. They are never so happy as when they are locked in combat, preferably with enemies outside the church; but if they can't find any there, then inside the church will be just fine. That kind of approach screams in the face of love and tears at the fabric of grace. Paul wants us to be reconcilers, involved in repairing relationships, not tearing them apart.

But at the same time, Paul is a realist. He is not talking about peace at the price of sacrificing truth or compromising principle. Furthermore, Paul is suggesting that there are circumstances where peace is impossible. Sometimes we have done everything in our power to establish peace, but the other person refuses. From his research and personal experience, Dr. Howard Hendricks concludes that in every church 16 percent of the members *will never change.*[9] They won't budge. They won't back down. They won't live in peace. What do we do when we hit that kind of brick wall? We realize that we are all responsible for our own actions, but we cannot be held responsible for the actions of others. Therefore, we are to do what we can, we are to attempt what is possible in the name of harmony, and then leave the consequences of the other person's actions and reactions to God. If disharmony and conflict continue, we should be sure we are not responsible for it.

• But let me say a word to you who refuse to allow the reconciliation process to go on. There has been a problem between you and someone else. An attempt at reconciliation has been initiated by the other person, but you've resisted. Why? Is it perhaps a remnant of pride . . . are you afraid that by being reconciled, you will have to admit to being partially at fault? Or, that you will no longer be able to blame the other person for your problems?

My friends, in the name of love, we have a responsibility to nurture reconciliation, even if that means we must act *sacrificially* toward those who hurt us. "But if your enemy is hungry, feed him, and if he is thirsty, give him a drink; for in so doing you will heap burning coals upon his head. Do not be overcome by evil, but overcome evil with good" (Romans 12:20-21).

It is not enough to merely refrain from seeking to inflict injury in return for injury; we are also to do positive good to those who have hurt us. To fail to do to our enemies the good they stand in need of, when it is in our power to do so, is a kind of indirect retaliation.

To illustrate precisely his point, Paul draws a picture of the ancient way of lighting fires. They obviously did not have matches in the first century and so, if they wanted to have a fire at home, they could go and borrow some coals from a neighbor. To do so, they took along an earthen jar to carry the coals. Now, if they happened to live next door to a good neighbor, he would fill the jar and you would carry it home on the top of your head. And that became a picture of an ample, generous response to a neighbor's need. It ultimately became a word picture for responding so generously to someone that he then felt ashamed of his attitude toward you. In fact, in the Book of Proverbs, the expression "coals of fire" symbolized a change of mind which took place as the result of an action of love.

When is the last time you behaved that way? Call to mind right now that person who is inflicting pain in your life. You may see them tomorrow at work or school, today at church, or this afternoon at home. Recall the painful event and the circumstances. Now recall your responses to them and weigh them in the balance of this text and in the name of love . . . and then promise to do better.

It was in a church in Munich that I saw him — a balding, heavyset man in a gray overcoat, a brown felt hat clutched between his hands. People were filing out of the basement room where I had just spoken, moving along the rows of wooden chairs to the door at the rear. It was 1947 and I had come from Holland to a defeated Germany with the message that God forgives.

The solemn faces stared back at me, not quite daring to believe. There were never questions after a talk in Germany in 1947. People stood up in silence, in silence collected their wraps, in silence left the room.

And that's when I saw him, working his way forward against the others. One moment I saw the overcoat and the brown hat; the next, a blue uniform and a visored cap with its skull and crossbones. It came back with a rush: the huge room with its harsh overhead lights; the pathetic pile of dresses and shoes in the center of the floor; the shame of walking naked past this man. I could see my sister's frail form ahead of me, ribs sharp beneath the parchment skin.

The place was Ravensbruck and the man who was making his way forward had been a guard — one of the most cruel guards.

Now he was in front of me, hand thrust out: "A fine message, Fraulein! How good it is to know that, as you say, all our sins are at the bottom of the sea!"

And I, who had spoken so glibly of forgiveness, fumbled in my pocketbook rather than take that hand. He would not remember me, of course — how could he remember one prisoner among those thousands of women?

But I remembered him and the leather crop swinging from his belt. I was face-to-face with one of my captors and my blood seemed to freeze.

"You mentioned Ravensbruck in your talk," he was saying. "I was a guard there." No, he did not remember me.

"But since that time," he went on, "I have become a Christian. I know that God has forgiven me for the cruel things I did there, but I would like to hear it from your lips as well. Fraulein," — again the hand came out — "will you forgive me?"

And I stood there — I whose sins had again and again to be forgiven — and could not forgive.

It could not have been many seconds that he stood there — hand held out — but to me it seemed hours as I wrestled with the most difficult thing I had ever had to do.

For I had to do it — I knew that. The message that God forgives has a prior condition: that we forgive those who have injured us. It was as simple and as horrible as that. And still I stood there with the coldness clutching my heart.

And so woodenly, mechanically I thrust my hand into the one stretched out to me. And as I did, an incredible thing took place. The current started in my shoulder, raced down my arm, and sprang into our joined hands. And then this healing warmth seemed to flood my whole being, bringing tears to my eyes.

"I forgive you, brother," I cried. "With all my heart!"

For a long moment we grasped each other's hands, the former guard and the former prisoner. I had never known God's love so intensely as I did then.[10]

11
THE DEBT OF LOVE

Owe nothing to anyone
except to love one another;
for he who loves his neighbor has fulfilled the law.
For this, "You shall not commit adultery,
you shall not murder, You shall not steal,
You shall not covet," and if there is
any other commandment, it is summed up
in this saying, "You shall love your neighbor
as yourself." Love does no wrong to a neighbor;
love therefore is the fulfillment of the law.

And this do, knowing the time,
that it is already the hour for you to awaken
from sleep; for now salvation is nearer to us
than when we believed. The night is almost gone,
and the day is at hand. Let us therefore lay aside
the deeds of darkness and put on the armor
of light. Let us behave properly as in the day,
not in carousing and drunkenness,
not in sexual promiscuity and sensuality,
not in strife and jealousy.
But put on the Lord Jesus Christ,
and make no provision for the flesh
in regard to its lusts.

Romans 13:8-14

Gayle Sayers was perhaps the best running back the Chicago Bears ever had. He was black. Brian Piccolo was the other running back, also a good athlete. He was white. That was nothing new, not even back in 1967. Blacks and whites often played on the same professional teams. But these two were different. They were roommates on the road—a first for race relations in football.

Gayle Sayers had never before had a close relationship with any white man, with the exception perhaps, of George Halas, the head coach of the Bears. And Brian Piccolo admitted that he had never known a black person ... not really.

But within the span of two brief years, 1967–69, their relationship deepened into one of the most memorable friendships in the history of sports. As the movie *Brian's Song* graphically portrayed, these two men truly loved each other.

Part of the reason they grew so close was the tragic fact that Brian Piccolo contracted cancer during the 1969 season. Although he fought to play the season out, he was in the hospital more than he was on the field. As the disease refused to go away, Sayers frequently flew in to be beside his friend. In time, the smell of death became increasingly more obvious, although the two of them, winners through and through, refused to surrender.

They and their wives had longstanding plans to sit together at the annual Professional Football Writer's Banquet in New York, where Gayle Sayers was to receive the George S. Halas award as "the most courageous player in professional football." By the time of the banquet, Brian Piccolo was too sick to attend. He was confined to his bed at home. As Gayle Sayers stood to his feet to receive the award, amid the resounding applause of the audience, tears began to flow which he could not restrain. Then he said these words: "You flatter me by giving me this award, but I tell you here and now that I accept it for Brian Piccolo. Brian Piccolo is the man of courage who should receive the George S. Halas award. I *love* Brian Piccolo and I'd like you to love him too. Tonight, when you hit your knees, please ask God to love him too."

How often do we hear adult men say, "I love you"? It is a remarkable and rare statement. Sayers and Piccolo had cultivated more than a superficial tough-guy relationship. Although they were rugged, heterosexual, competitive men to the core, an *authentic love* had developed between these two strong athletes.[1]

It's the very kind of love that the Apostle Paul brings to our viewing screen in Romans 13, beginning with verse 8: "Owe nothing to anyone except to love one another; for he who loves his neighbor has fulfilled the law."

It has been said, "The most dangerous thing in the world is not to be weak — we all manage to survive the ludicrous weakness and inadequacy of our infancy: the most dangerous thing in the world is to be *unloved*."[2]

Psychiatrist Dr. William Glasser, in his classic text *Reality Therapy*, says that "psychiatry must be concerned with two basic psychological needs: (1) the need to feel that we are worthwhile to ourselves and others, and (2) the need to love and to be loved."[3]

But long before *Reality Therapy* came to public attention, the Apostle Paul addressed our need to love and be loved. In this passage, he slips in through the back door by first of all talking about our financial debt-load. Now please understand that Paul is not forbidding borrowing. He is saying that the Christian should not leave his debts unpaid, but should take care of them in a timely manner. Few things bring greater embarrassment to the Christian community than the accumulation of debts and the refusal to pay them. As Christians, then, we have a responsibility to keep short accounts.

But that is not the primary message here because Paul goes on to talk about a debt that we must pay every day, and yet will never be able to pay off. And that's the debt of love.

We might pay off our Visa bill in January, if we're lucky. We might even at some time pay off our mortgage. But we can never say, "I have paid off the debt of love." In other words, love is a permanent obligation. Whatever else we do, we are to love.

One of the early fathers of the church, a man by the name of Origen who lived around A.D. 200, had this to say about verse 8: "So Paul desires that our debt of love should remain and never cease to be owed; for it is expedient that we should both pay this debt daily and (yet) always owe it."[4]

So what does that mean to us? Simply that we are to see ourselves as debtors to everyone. Everytime we meet someone we ought to say to ourselves, "I need to show love. I have a great and wonderful debt to pay." When we rub shoulders with people, we must remember that our first obligation is to love them, to show courtesy, kindness, patience, understanding ... whatever it takes, whatever the situation demands. It is a debt that we owe.

This kind of love is the giving of self for no reason other than the satisfaction of giving of self and for the contentment it brings. This is a unique and special characteristic

of . . . love. This kind of love's generosity needs no rec-
ompense, no pat on the head, no tit-for-tat balance and
no reward. . . . This kind of love and generous giving of
self happens because it must happen. . . . In this kind of
love — feelings, time, thoughts, and energy are given, are
received, and are exchanged. But exchange is not the
motivating force. Exchange takes place as a natural consequence; who gets more, less, or what, is of no consequence at all.[5]

That's a switch, isn't it? Frequently in our relationships we
are intensely concerned with what we get out of the deal,
and far less occupied with what we give. And then when
we don't get what we have set our sights on, we are bent
out of shape and either sulk or complain about it. What's
worse, we keep score, keep track of how others "love us,"
whether we're getting our fair shake. But that kind of
warped thinking sours love, because it runs from the meaning of true biblical love. Quit keeping score. Don't worry
about who's winning. Paul is saying that our emphasis
should be on giving, not receiving.

Remember, we can judge how far we have risen on the
scale of life by asking ourselves one question: How wisely
and how deeply do I care? To be Christianized is to be
sensitized, for Christians are people who care. No one, any-
where, can come into authentic contact with Jesus Christ
without beginning to care.

PAY THE DEBT OF LOVE

We have a debt to pay. That's the general principle, but if
you've paid any attention to the pen of Paul, you'd know
that he was not given to generalities. He insisted on pin-
ning us to the wall with specifics . . . of how to's. And in
verse 9, he begins to do just that: " 'You shall not commit
adultery, you shall not murder, you shall not steal, you shall
not covet,' and if there is any other commandment, it is

summed up in this saying, 'You shall love your neighbor as yourself.' "

Paul informs us that if we consistently love other people, we fulfill or complete the law of Scripture. What does that mean? Well, in verse 9, Paul lists four of the Ten Commandments. He omits those commandments which refer to God and concentrates on the ones that tie us to people. He wants to emphasize that all the commandments which impact our relationships with others can be summarized under the one commandment, "Love your neighbor as yourself." The basic rules of life that make possible relationships of trust are gathered up into that one most basic commandment.

But let's put this in terms we can't miss. What we are being told about love is this: Love will not sleep with a neighbor's wife or husband, or even flirt with them. Love will not murder a neighbor—physically or verbally. Love will not poison a neighbor's dog, or throw garbage over the fence into his backyard, or leave trash cans out on the street for six days. Love will not steal from a neighbor, or even keep his lawn mower or snowblower more than a month. Love will not covet what belongs to a neighbor, it won't drool over his home if it is larger than yours, or stew about his new car or interior remodeling. Love does not want what a neighbor has, but rejoices with him over what he has.

You can test yourself very easily in this area. How do you react when:

• a friend excitedly tells you of his/her promotion or new job, while you flounder at the same position for years, or even visit the lines of the unemployed?

• you overhear another woman being complimented on her beauty and weight?

• you see report cards of children with straight A's and the only thing your kid knows about an "A" is that it's the first letter of the alphabet?

• your raise is smaller than that of a coworker who

doesn't work as hard as you do?

You see how we fight against the debt of love. Charles Finney, in his book, *Principles of Love,* does a masterful job exposing the raw edges of our selfishness.

> Selfishness is a phenomenon of the will, and consists in committing the will to the gratification of [your] desires. Selfishness begins when the will yields to the desire and seeks to obey it in opposition to the law . . . of God. It matters not what kind of desire it is; if it is the desire that governs the will, this is selfishness.[6]

Paul is suggesting that our love for each other may be a more easily recognizable measure of where we stand with God, than our declared love for God. It is possible to fake love for God and to fool ourselves and others, but it is excruciatingly difficult to fake love for others. The moment we try, we break out in a cold sweat and people observe that something isn't right. So our love for others provides a helpful internal measure of our spiritual state.

Sarah Sterling, in a piece entitled, "A Friend Like You," seems to put all this all together when she pens:

Everyone needs a friend like you.

You found me lying on your doorstep
with broken wings, covered with dirt.
   Like a torn up piece of cloth
   Like a battered old toy
   Like a gaping, ugly sore
   That hurts even to look at
     or touch
     or care about.

Alone
Afraid
Injured
And yet you opened the door and gently let me in.

You bandaged the wounds

And soothed the raw edges where it hurt the most
You set my broken bones in place
And pieced back together my shattered dreams.
What I thought was the end
Was really
The beginning.

You invited me on a journey . . .

The warmth in your smile
And the care in your eyes told me I was safe.

But . . . I tire so easily
   And I'm really not very brave
   And I'm not sure just exactly where it is I'm going
Or just what I'll find once I get there.

Then I took one step . . .
As if to believe you really are there.
. . . and then I see you mean what you say.
You do care.

You held my hand across the rough places
And gave me a boost over the high fences
You let me run free across the fields
Always there
Always with me
Even if I ran ahead
Or tagged behind
Always gently pursuing me to go on

Yet totally accepting me right where I was . . .
   on the rocks
   on the fence
   in the mud
   up a tree
   in the field

Along the way you teach me things . . .

how to cry—so I won't be afraid to hurt
how to get up—so I won't be afraid to fall
how to love—so I won't be afraid to give.

My injuries are healing
My soul is awakening
My eyes are not afraid to look at
    where I've been
    where I am
    where I'm going

Even though I'm unsure of where I am now

I'll walk on with you.
I trust your outstretched arms and your faithful carings.
Thank you for mending my broken heart
For soothing my aches
hearing my cries
    understanding my pain
        sharing my grief.

How [blest] I am!

Everyone needs a friend like you![7]

DO NO WRONG TO YOUR NEIGHBOR

Paul's next specific focus is found in verse 10: "Love does no wrong to a neighbor; love therefore is the fulfillment of the law."

Now understand that the phrase "does no wrong" doesn't suggest for a second that there are never occasions in your relationships when there will not be pain, hurt, confrontation, or reprimand. If you try to define love without those elements, you set yourself up for incredible disillusionment and ultimate bitterness.

What Paul is saying is that *love does not purposely set out to cause pain or intentionally plot harm for others.* If you're acting in love, you don't go to work to consciously do or say something that will inflict pain. You make every effort to avoid that kind of action.

Yet, I sometimes wonder if that is true. I have a sinking feeling that we don't shoot straight on this one; I wonder if we think our situation is so different, so unique, that injecting pain is justified. John Chrysostom, a great preacher of the fourth century, said it well, but with a catch of sadness, when he wrote of the church: "For this I grieve, that, living among brethren, we need to be on our guard against injury. For this reason one may find many who trust pagans sooner than Christians."[8]

So often Christian love is made laughable because those of us who are loudest in our praise of love, and confident that we are demonstrating it, persist in injuring others.

How about you? If you were royally ticked this week about something or someone, what did you say? What did you do? Society continues to program us to strike back, the quicker the better in most cases. "Get them before they get you." We have fallen for the pattern of revenge. We believe we have every right to strike back because of what they did to us.

But that kind of behavior does not make payments on the debt of love. Instead, it overdraws our account. It learns our secret number and arrives at the automatic teller of our lives and bankrupts our personal relationships. And it is not where Paul would have us go. The point that leaps from this page is how absolutely irresistible Christianity would be *in everyday life* if Christians loved their neighbors. If we would consistently see ourselves as debtors to love, think how the Gospel would spread.

LIVE AS PEOPLE OF GOD

If that is not reason enough to act in love, Paul concludes this passage of Scripture by citing two additional reasons.

The first focuses on the *age* we live in and the *time* it represents: "And this do, knowing the time, that it is already the hour for you to awaken from sleep; for now salvation is nearer to us than when we believed. The night is almost gone, and the day is at hand" (vv. 11-12). The phrase in verse 12, "the day is at hand," is a reference to the second coming of Jesus Christ to this planet, when He will return as Lord and King. The same thought is expressed in verse 11 in the words, "Salvation is nearer to us than when we believed."

To be sure, salvation is already an accomplished fact for those of us who have accepted Jesus Christ as our personal Savior from sin. And as an achieved or accomplished fact, it has continuing results of forgiveness to this present moment. But our salvation also has a future and final aspect — which will occur at the second coming of Christ, for at that moment our faith in Jesus Christ will be finally rewarded in the sense that we will be delivered out of this world and into eternity with Christ. For the Christian, the promise of the return of Christ is supposed to hover over us and motivate us to act in love. It apparently wasn't having that effect in Paul's day and so, in effect, he said, "Let's get with the program, folks. It's time to wake up — don't waste another minute."

I love the way the Amplified Bible expresses this verse: "Besides this you know what a critical hour this is, how it is high time for you to wake up out of your sleep — rouse to reality. For salvation (our final deliverance) is nearer to us now than when we first believed in Christ."

Paul is shouting, "Love your neighbor as yourself," but do it not only because the law of Christ demands this, but especially because you know how very critical is the time in which we are now living."

The people of the first century were convinced that Christ could return in their lifetime. Paul hitchhiked on that belief to remind them and us that Christ's return *ought to make a difference in the way we live.* We don't have all the time in the world. Each ache, each pain, each gray hair, each new wrinkle, each funeral, is a reminder that it's later than it has ever been before. So, let's get with it!

But getting with it is more than just talk. Look at verses 12 and 13: "Let us therefore lay aside the deeds of darkness and put on the armor of light. Let us behave properly as in the day, not in carousing and drunkenness, not in sexual promiscuity and sensuality, not in strife and jealousy."

Acting in love is not only ministering and caring for others. There is also a cost in our lifestyle; that is what Paul is driving home here. Love *does* what nobody else is doing— it cares, it reaches out. But also, love *does not do* what everybody else is doing. *The Living Bible* paraphrases these verses: "So quit the evil deeds of darkness and put on the armor of right living, as we who live in the daylight should. Be decent and true in everything so that all can approve your behavior. Don't spend your time in wild parties and getting drunk or in adultery and lust, or fighting and jealousy."

Paul lays his cards on the table, doesn't he? He talks about "carousing and drunkenness." Those words together picture some lush out having a good time, grabbing for all the gusto and disturbing people in the process. The Christian who wants to demonstrate love must set aside that pattern of behavior.

Think about this. Alcohol is one of our nation's major health problems, costing the United States about $120 billion a year. Paul Harvey recently reported that Americans spend $28 billion annually on alcohol and another $35 billion counteracting its effects. The grain used in producing alcoholic beverages, if used in food, could eliminate a major portion of the world's hunger problem.[9]

Alcohol consumption is the prime cause of violence, intentional or unintentional, in our society, and it is more often than not the motivator for sexual abuse by men of women and children.[10]

Love runs from that, as well as from what Paul terms "sexual promiscuity and sensuality." "Sexual promiscuity" means going to bed with someone other than your husband or wife. "Sensuality" goes even further. One linguist said that it is "shameless greed, sheer self-indulgence which is such a slave to its so-called pleasures that it lost to shame. It is a person who acknowledges no restraints."[11]

My friends, our God has graciously provided the gift of intimacy for husbands and wives. Sex is not sinful. God designed it. But He designed it for a context. Listen to Billy Graham's good word here:

> One thing the Bible does not teach is that sex in itself is sin. Far from being prudish, the Bible celebrates sex and its proper use, presenting it as God-created, God-or-dained, God-blessed. It makes plain that God Himself implanted the physical magnetism between the sexes for [at least] two reasons: for the propagation of the human race, and for the expression of that kind of love between man and wife that makes for true oneness. His command to the first man and woman to be "one flesh" was as important as His command to "be fruitful and multiply."[12]

Sexual intimacy in all its variety and joy is a gift from heaven for marriage, and in that context, it walks with love. Outside of that context, it violates love.

But Paul goes on. Right alongside drunkenness and immorality, he adds "strife and jealousy." They too fight against love. "Strife" is a word that wears boxing gloves. It describes someone who lives to quarrel and fight. "Jealousy" digs deeper and refers to the kind of zeal which does not try to help but rather to harm, so that you come out ahead. Both words indicate a determination to have your own way. Jealousy is narcissistic selfishness in its purest form. Jealousy is never even related to love. In fact, love simply cannot flourish where jealousy exists.

Strife and jealousy perfectly describe someone who cannot stand being surpassed and who begrudges others their success and position. And it is amazing how many Christians engage in this as if it were their calling from God—keeping others down, making sure they stay in their place, reveling in conversations that divide, that dismantle people's character. None of that can coexist with loving others. And Paul says we must put them off.

EMBRACE THE LORD EVERY DAY

We have work to do, not only in negative areas, but also in a more positive one. "But put on the Lord Jesus Christ, and make no provision for the flesh in regard to its lusts" (v. 14). Dr. Ray Stedman does such a good job explaining this verse:

> When I get up in the morning I put on my clothes, intending them to be part of me all day, to go where I go and do what I do. They cover me and make me presentable to others. That is the purpose of clothes. In the same way, the apostle is saying to us, 'Put on Jesus Christ when you get up in the morning. Make Him a part of your life that day. Intend that He go with you everywhere you go, and that He act through you in everything you do. Call upon His resources. Live your life in Christ.[13]

From the looks of people on Sunday mornings, I'd say they had spent a good deal of time selecting what to wear. But on the other side, it's apparent that some of them don't see that well. Paul is suggesting that we daily spend as much time thinking of Christ and His impact on our lives as we do in picking out our clothes in the morning.

To put on the Lord Jesus Christ means to embrace Him again and again, in faith and confidence, in grateful loyalty and obedience. Making payments on our debt of love comes by putting off the deeds of darkness and putting on Christ. That is something we must constantly do. No onetime public statement or dedication, no matter how wonderful, will do the trick. Christ must be put on regularly, if we would love regularly.

Can you imagine what would happen to your church, if

each one of us chose to practice this text in our lives? Can
you imagine what would happen to our city? I don't think
we have a comprehension of what could happen . . . if we
would truly live out the debt of love.

It was Sunday, Christmas. Our family had spent the holi-
days in San Francisco with my husband's parents. But in
order for us to be back at work on Monday, we found
ourselves driving the 400 miles back home to Los Angeles on Christmas Day.

We stopped for lunch in King City. The restaurant was
nearly empty. We were the only family and ours were
the only children. I heard Erik, my one-year-old, squeal
with glee: "Hi there." "Hi there." He pounded his fat
baby hands — whack, whack — on the metal high chair
tray. His face was alive with excitement, eyes wide, gums
bared in a toothless grin. He wriggled, and chirped, and
giggled, and then I saw the source of his merriment . . .
and my eyes could not take it all in at once.

A tattered rag of a coat obviously bought by someone
else eons ago — dirty, greasy, and worn . . . baggy pants —
spindly body — toes that poked out of would-be
shoes . . . a shirt that had ring-around-the-collar all over
and a face like none other . . . gums as bare as Erik's.

"Hi there, baby; hi there, big boy. I see ya, buster."

My husband and I exchanged a look that was a cross
between "What do we do?" and "Poor devil."

Our meal came, and the cacaphony continued. Now
the old bum was shouting from across the room: "Do ya
know patty cake? Atta boy . . . Do ya know peek-a-boo?
Hey, look, he knows peek-a-boo!"

Eric continued to laugh and answer, "Hi there." Every
call was echoed. Nobody thought it was cute. The guy
was a drunk and a disturbance. I was embarrassed. My
husband, Dennis, was humiliated. Even our six-year-old
said, "Why is that old man talking so loud?"

Dennis went to pay the check, imploring me to get
Erik and meet him in the parking lot. "Lord, just let me
out of here before he speaks to me or Erik." I bolted for
the door.

It soon was obvious that both the Lord and Erik had other plans. As I drew closer to the man, I turned my back, walking to sidestep him—and any air he might be breathing. As I did so, Erik, all the while with his eyes riveted to his best friend, leaned far over my arm, reaching with both arms to a baby's "pick me up" position.

In a split second of balancing my baby and turning to counter his weight I came eye to eye with the old man. Erik was lunging for him, arms spread wide.

The bum's eyes both asked and implored, "Would you let me hold your baby?"

There was no need for me to answer since Erik propelled himself from my arms to the man's. Suddenly a very old man and very young baby consummated their love relationship. Erik laid his tiny head upon the man's ragged shoulder. The man's eyes closed, and I saw tears hover beneath his lashes. His aged hands full of grime, and pain, and hard labor—gently, so gently, cradled my baby's bottom and stroked his back.

I stood awestruck. The old man rocked and cradled Erik in his arms for a moment, and then his eyes opened and set squarely on mine. He said in a firm commanding voice, "You take care of this baby."

Somehow I managed, "I will," from a throat that contained a stone.

He pried Erik from his chest—unwillingly, longingly—as though he was in pain.

I held my arms open to receive my baby and again the gentleman addressed me.

"God bless you, ma'am. You've given me my Christmas gift."

I said nothing more than a muttered thanks.

With Erik back in my arms, I ran for the car. Dennis wondered why I was crying and holding Erik so tightly and why I was saying, "My God, my God, forgive me."[14]

12
MISSING NO LONGER

*See how great a love the Father has bestowed upon us,
that we should be called children of God; and such we are.
For this reason the world does not know us, because
it did not know Him. Beloved, now we are children of God,
and it has not appeared as yet what we shall be. We know that,
when He appears, we shall be like Him, because we shall see Him
just as He is. And every one who has this hope fixed
on Him purifies himself, just as He is pure.*

*Every one who practices sin also practices lawlessness;
and sin is lawlessness. And you know that He appeared
in order to take away sins; and in Him there is no sin.
No one who abides in Him sins; no one who sins has seen Him
or known Him. Little children, let no one deceive you;
the one who practices righteousness is righteous, just as
He is righteous; the one who practices sin is of the devil;
for the devil has sinned from the beginning. The Son of God
appeared for this purpose, that He might destroy the works
of the devil. No one who is born of God practices sin, because
His seed abides in him; and he cannot sin,
because he is born of God.*

*By this the children of God and the children of the devil
are obvious: any one who does not practice righteousness
is not of God, nor the one who does not love his brother.
For this is the message which you have heard from the beginning,
that we should love one another; not as Cain, who was of
the evil one, and slew his brother. And for what reason
did he slay him? Because his deeds were evil,
and his brother's were righteous. Do not marvel, brethren,
if the world hates you.*

*We know that we have passed out of death into life,
because we love the brethren. He who does not love
abides in death. Every one who hates his brother is a murderer;
and you know that no murderer has eternal life abiding in him.*

*We know love by this, that He laid down His life for us,
and we ought to lay down our lives for the brethren. But whoever
has the world's goods, and beholds his brother in need
and closes his heart against him, how does the love of God
abide in him? Little children, let us not love with word
or with tongue, but in deed and truth. We shall know by this
that we are of the truth, and shall assure our heart before Him,
in whatever our heart condemns us; for God is greater
than our heart, and knows all things.*

*Beloved, if our heart does not condemn us, we have confidence
before God; and whatever we ask we receive from Him,
because we keep His commandments and do the things that are
pleasing in His sight. And this is His commandment,
that we believe in the name of His Son Jesus Christ,
and love one another, just as He commanded us. And the one
who keeps His commandments abides in Him, and He in him.
And we know by this that He abides in us, by the Spirit which
He has given us. Beloved, do not believe every spirit,
but test the spirits to see whether they are from God; because
many false prophets have gone out into the world. By this
you know the Spirit of God: every spirit that confesses
that Jesus Christ has come in the flesh is from God;
and every spirit that does not confess Jesus is not from God;
and this is the spirit of the antichrist, of which you have heard
that it is coming, and now it is already in the world. You are
from God, little children, and have overcome them;
because greater is He who is in you than he who is in the world.
They are from the world; therefore they speak as from the world,
and the world listens to them. We are from God; he who knows
God listens to us; he who is not from God does not listen to us.
By this we know the spirit of truth and the spirit of error.*

Beloved, let us love one another, for love is from God;
and every one who loves is born of God and knows God.
The one who does not love does not know God, for God is love.

By this the love of God was manifested in us, that God sent
His only begotten Son into the world so that we might live
through Him. In this is love, not that we loved God, but that
He loved us and sent His Son to be the propitiation for our sins.

Beloved, if God so loved us, we also ought to love one another.
No one has beheld God at any time; if we love one another,
God abides in us, and His love is perfected in us. By this
we know that we abide in Him and He in us, because He has
given us of His Spirit. And we have beheld and bear witness
that the Father has sent the Son to be the Savior of the world.
Whoever confesses that Jesus is the Son of God,
God abides in him, and he in God.

And we have come to know and have believed the love
which God has for us. God is love, and the one who abides
in love abides in God, and God abides in him. By this,
love is perfected with us, that we may have confidence
in the day of judgment; because as He is, so also are
we in this world.

There is no fear in love; but perfect love casts out fear,
because fear involves punishment, and the one who fears
is not perfected in love. We love, because He first loved us.

If some one says, "I love God," and hates his brother, he is a liar;
for the one who does not love his brother whom he has seen,
cannot love God whom he has not seen. And this commandment
we have from Him, that the one who loves God
should love his brother also.

1 John 3–4

He did it to me again! Just when I thought I knew what to expect, he did it to me again! With the simple flex of his wrist and the trail of his pen, he did it . . . he made me laugh and then he made me cry. Just like he will do it to you. Listen for your heartbeat as Robert Fulghum speaks for many of us:

The cardboard box is marked "THE GOOD STUFF." . . . The box contains those odds and ends of personal treasures that have survived many bouts of clean-it-out-and-throw-it-away that seize me from time to time. A thief looking into the box would not take anything — he couldn't get a dime for any of it. But if the house ever catches on fire, the box goes with me when I run.

One of the keepsakes in the box is a small paper bag. Lunch size. Though the top is sealed with duct tape, staples, and several paper clips, there is a ragged rip in one side through which the contents may be seen. This particular lunch sack has been in my care for maybe fourteen years. But it really belongs to my daughter, Molly. Soon after she came of school age, she became an enthusiastic participant in packing the morning lunches. One morning Molly handed me two bags as I was about to leave. One regular lunch sack. And the one with the duct tape and staples and paper clips. "Why two bags?"

"The other one is something else." "What's in it?" "Just some stuff—take it with you."

At midday, while hurriedly scarfing down my real lunch, I tore open Molly's bag and shook out the contents. Two hair ribbons, three small stones, a plastic dinosaur, a pencil stub, a tiny seashell, two animal crackers, a marble, a used lipstick, a small doll, two chocolate kisses, and thirteen pennies.

I smiled. How charming. Rising to hustle off to all the important business of the afternoon, I swept the desk clean—into the wastebasket—leftover lunch, Molly's junk, and all. There wasn't anything in there I needed.

That evening Molly came to stand beside me while I was reading the paper. "Where's my bag?" "What bag?" "You know, the one I gave you this morning." "I left it at the office, why?" "I forgot to put this note in it." She hands over the note. "Besides, I want it back." "Why?" "Those are my things in the sack, Daddy, the ones I really like—I thought you might like to play with them, but now I want them back. You didn't lose the bag, did you, Daddy?" Tears puddled in her eyes. . . "Bring it tomorrow, Okay?" "Sure thing—don't worry." As she hugged my neck with relief, I unfolded the note that had not got into the sack: "I love you, Daddy."

Oh. And also—uh-oh.

Molly had given me her treasures. All that a seven-year-old held dear. LOVE IN A PAPER SACK. And I had missed it. Not only missed it, but had thrown it in the wastebasket because "there wasn't anything in there I needed." Dear God.

It was a long trip back to the office. But there was nothing else to be done. Just ahead of the janitor, I picked up the wastebasket and poured the contents on my desk . . . and found the jewels.

After washing the mustard off the dinosaurs and spraying the whole thing with breath-freshener to kill the smell of onions, I carefully smoothed out the wadded ball of brown paper into a semifunctional bag and put the treasures inside and carried the whole thing home gingerly, like an injured kitten. The next evening I returned it to Molly, no questions asked, no explanations offered. After dinner I asked her to tell me about the stuff in the sack. It took a long time to tell. Everything had a story, a memory, or was attached to dreams and imaginary friends.

To my surprise, Molly gave the bag to me once again, several days later. Same ratty bag. Same stuff inside. I felt forgiven. And trusted. *And loved.* Over several months the bag went with me from time to time. It was never clear to me why I did or did not get it on a given day. I began to think of it as the Daddy Prize and tried to be good the night before so I might be given it the next morning.

In time Molly turned her attention to other things . . . found other treasures . . . lost interest in the game . . . grew up. Something. Me? I was left holding the bag. She gave it to me one morning and never asked for its return. And so I have it still.

Sometimes I think of all the times in this sweet life when I must have missed the affection I was being given. A friend calls this "standing knee-deep in the river and dying of thirst." So the worn paper sack is there in the box. Left over from a time when a child said, "Here, this is the best I've got. Take it, it's yours. Such as I have, give I to thee." I MISSED IT THE FIRST TIME. BUT IT'S MY BAG NOW.[1]

It's probably true for you — I know it is for me — that all too often we find the empty lunch bags of our past blowing across the back lots of our lives. Crumpled, torn, and empty . . . we see them dance by so close and we run after them to retrieve them, but the wind is too strong, too relentless and they seem to stay always out of reach.

FIND THE SOURCE OF LOVE

But it doesn't have to be that way. Oh, I'm not going to suggest we can all go back and magically recapture all the lunch-bag experiences of love in our life. Sometimes that's possible, but not often. What I am suggesting is that we can begin today to start a new collection, our own collection that we give to others. The Apostle John says it simply but very clearly: "Beloved, let us love one another, for love is from God; and everyone who loves is born of God and knows God. . . . And this commandment we have from Him, that the one who loves God should love his brother also" (1 John 4:7, 21).

Does it seem strange to think of love in terms of a commandment? That is too regimented, almost military. Maybe, until you remember that we are dealing with biblical love . . . the Greek word is "agape." Agape love is volitional, not emotional. That is, it is riveted to the mind, to the will. It is a decision we make, as opposed to a feeling that overcomes us. That is why it can be commanded. You cannot command feelings, but by an active determination the will can be commanded. Agape love works for the good of another person. When John talks about it here, he does so within a CONTINUING mode. His idea is not that love is a one-shot deal, a flash in the pan, a quick fix. That's not where John is headed. Love is a determined way of life. Love is an *activity*, not a passive effect; it is a *standing in,* not a falling for. Love primarily *gives* rather than receives.

Love is a principle by which we deliberately live. It's a directional tone in our lives. Under the banner, "Your Life Will Be Richer — IF," an unknown author suggests:

> Your life will be richer — if on this day you will make an effort to: mend a quarrel. Search for a forgotten friend. Dismiss a suspicion and replace it with trust. Write a letter to someone who misses you. Encourage someone who has lost faith. Keep a promise. Forget an old grudge. Examine your demands on others, and vow to reduce them. Fight for a principle. Express your gratitude. Overcome an old fear . . . tell someone you love him. Tell him again. And again. And again.

That is fulfilling the commandment of love. But don't imagine you can simply flip a switch, phone in an order, and have love delivered into your life. Love is not a product to be marketed, nor a commodity to be used until it runs out. Love is a way of life which finds its source in God: "Beloved, let us love one another, for love is from God; and everyone who loves is born of God and knows God. The one who does not love does not know God, for God is love. By this the love of God was manifested in us, that God has sent His only begotten Son into the world so that we might live through Him. In this is love, not that we loved God, but that He loved us and sent His Son to be the propitiation for our sins. Beloved, if God so loved us, we also ought to love one another" (1 John 4:7-11).

God is the originator of love. Agape love exists in our lives *only* as a response to God's initial love for us. John tells us that all of God's activity is loving activity. That's what he means in verse 8 when he says, "God is love." In other words, if God creates, He creates in love. If He rules, He rules in love. If He judges, He judges in love.

But we need to understand that in saying, "God is love," John is *not* saying, "Love is God." That is not a biblical idea. As John makes clear, the controlling principle of the universe is not an abstract quality of love, but a sovereign, living God who is the source of all love. And God's love, like ours, involves action. It involves giving. God's love required Him to send Jesus Christ, the visible proof of the Father's love for the world. This is not simply because He showed up on this piece of real estate we call the earth, but because of what He did when He showed up. Let's look at verse 16 of 1 John 3, so that we can link it with verses 9 and 10 of chapter 4: "We know love by this, that He laid down His life for us; and we ought to lay down our lives for the brethren."

God sent Jesus Christ to die so that we might live. Whether we like it or not, the Bible informs us that we are separated from God because of our sin. Don't look to pass this sin off to somebody else; just look at your own life, your own sin that separates you from a holy God. In order for that separation to cease, our sin has to be erased or covered. Christ's death provides that covering. In fact, that's what 1 John 4:10 says. The word *propitiation* means "a covering." Christ's death covers your sins. But it does more — it satisfies a holy God. You see, when sin is present, God's holiness and justice demand that a penalty be paid, a sentence be passed. The penalty for sin is eternal death apart from God in hell. And there is no way that you and I can change that. There's no higher court of appeal. No attorney to buy off. No witness to bribe or juror to lobby. We are dead to rights. But then Jesus Christ steps in and becomes our "propitiation" — our covering and our satisfaction. Christ's death did just that. He paid the penalty for our sins and satisfied God's demand for justice. And as a result, you and I can be connected with God. We are able to live eternally with God; we can now demonstrate God's love. God's demonstration of love is our source of love.

> This then, is the wonder of the Christian message: that God is this kind of God; that He loves me with a love that is not turned off by my sins, my failures, my inadequacies. . . . I am not a miserable offender cowering under the glare of an angry deity. I am a man loved by God Himself. I have touched the very heart of the universe, and have found His name to be love. And that love has reached me, not because I have merited God's favor, not because I have anything to boast about, but because of what He is, and because of what Christ has done for me in the Father's name. . . .[2]

Rag Doll

> Lord, I come to you like a broken rag doll,
> My dress is torn and stained.
> My arm is half-hanging on.
> My eyes aren't shining and trusting like
>   they once were.
> And my expression isn't innocent
>   and transparent anymore.

I'm not the unused, brand-new rag doll
    I once was.

Yes, my smile is still there,
But not as spontaneous as it once was;
It's a little more forced now;
A bit more tired.

I need to be picked up by you, Lord,
Picked up
    held tightly
      loved
        and reassured.

Reassured that no matter how I look,
Or how dirty and scuffed up and
    broken I am,
You love me just like when I was
    brand-new.

Would you please hold me, Lord?

Robin Williams

ACTIVELY PURSUE LOVE

"We know that we have passed out of death into life, because we love the brethren. He who does not love abides in
death. Everyone who hates his brother is a murderer; and
you know that no murderer has eternal life abiding in him"
(1 John 3:14-15). "The one who does not love does not
know God, for God is love. . . . If someone says, 'I love
God,' and hates his brother, he is a liar; for the one who
does not love his brother whom he has seen, cannot love
God whom he has not seen" (4:8, 20).

These are incredibly sober verses. John begins by informing us that the mark of spiritual life is love. Love for others then results because we are connected to God through Christ. To be unable or unwilling to love means that a person is without spiritual life from God the Father and remains in death or separation from God.

Furthermore, when love is consistently absent in a person's life, knowledge of God does not exist. A failure to love can only mean that a person has no true knowledge of God, and never even began to get acquainted with Him. All God's activity is loving activity; therefore a stranger to love is a stranger to God.

There is an old French proverb that says: "What! No star, and you are going out to sea? Marching, and you have no music? Traveling, and you have no book? What! No love, and you are going out to live?"

A person who refuses to demonstrate biblical love does not know God and is not alive spiritually. For you see, the nonloving state never stays neutral. Oh, you try to stay removed from people, and from relationships that entangle your heart. You pride yourself in not getting involved, but in reality, you're only fooling yourself, because those who do not actively love, sooner or later slide into another activity . . . an activity that, like acid, eats through the lunch-bag experiences of our life and that is *hate.*

Now before you swallow too hard, let me explain that the verb translated "hate" is in the present tense in the Greek language, which means it is descriptive of a continuing, chronic mind-set or attitude. It does not mean your momentary skirmishes with anger or distaste. It grapples instead with something that impacts you regularly. It is something that characterizes your life.

Hate is chronic, deep, abiding hostility that goes on and on — overflowing and polluting all aspects of our lives. It blocks and destroys all other feelings, but especially love. It contributes to bitterness and cynicism. It aids suspicion, paranoia, and bigotry. It is a destroyer of health, morale and creativity. More than anything, it cripples and distorts relationships, making love impossible.[3]

Dr. Lewis Smedes, in his book on forgiveness, drives to
the heart of hatred when he writes:

> There is an aggressive fury that drives us out of our wits.
> A woman wishes her former husband would catch [some
> disease], or at least be miserably unhappy with his new
> wife. You hope the friend who hurt you when he told
> your secret will get fired from the new job he found. We
> may settle for lesser retribution or we may wish our
> enemy would drop dead. In any case, we are not only
> drained of the positive energy to wish someone well, we
> devoutly wish them ill. We are poised to attack. This is
> aggressive hate.[4]

Aggressive hate repels love, and its twin sister sooner or
later appears: "Everyone who hates his brother is a murderer" (v. 15). John links hatred with murder, because in the
heart there is no difference. Hatred is the wish that the
other person was not there, the longing that he or she
might be dead.

To hate is to despise, to cut someone off from relationships; murder is simply the ultimate fulfillment of that attitude. If I constantly hate somebody, I am no different from
a murderer in my attitude, and that kind of hatred is incompatible with spiritual life. The person who hates has no life
in God, no rebirth, no fellowship, despite pleas to the
contrary.

John minces no words here. He doesn't speak so as to
confuse. His point is perfectly clear. If you cannot or will
not love, you are spiritually dead; you have no connection
with God. It doesn't matter what church you attend, whether you teach Sunday School, serve on a board or committee,
or sing in the choir. That does not cover for your lack of
love. And if you hate others . . . even if you feel it is justified hatred . . . if that hate is persistent, chronic . . . you are
as guilty before God as a murderer and you stand apart
from Him.

LEARN THE SACRIFICE OF LOVE

"We know love by this, that He laid down His life for us; and we ought to lay down our lives for the brethren" (1 John 3:16).

Christ's sacrificial death distinguishes agape love from all other loves by its cost. It cost Christ His life. But agape love is, in fact, the denial of self for another's gain. Love means the willingness to do anything for the other person. What this verse is teaching is that love must be prepared to meet the needs of others, whatever the cost in self-sacrifice.

What has your love for someone else cost you recently? Time? Inconvenience? Delay? Stress? Worry? In his book, *Mortal Lessons: Notes in the Art of Surgery,* Dr. Richard Selzer illustrates the self-sacrificing part of love:

> I stand by the bed where a young woman lies, her face postoperative, her mouth twisted in palsy, clownish. A tiny twig of the facial nerve, the one to the muscles of her mouth, has been severed. She will be thus from now on. The surgeon has followed with religious fervor the curve of her flesh; I promise you that. Nevertheless, to remove the tumor in her cheek, I had cut the little nerve.
>
> Her young husband is in the room. He stands on the opposite side of the bed, and together they seem to dwell in the evening lamplight, isolated from me, private. Who are they, I ask myself, he and this wry-mouth I have made, who gaze at and touch each other so generously, greedily? The young woman speaks.
>
> "Will my mouth always be like this?" she asks.
>
> "Yes," I say, "it will. It is because the nerve was cut."
>
> She nods, and is silent. But the young man smiles.
>
> "I like it," he says. "It is kind of cute."
>
> All at once I know who he is. I understand, and I lower my gaze. Unmindful, he bends to kiss her crooked mouth, and I so close can see how he twists his own lips to accommodate to hers, to show her that their kiss still works.[5]

In the event that you still find yourself distanced from the application of agape love, consider the second credential of love: "But whoever has the world's goods, and beholds his neighbor in need and closes his heart against him, how does the love of God abide in him?" (1 John 3:17) The phrase "the world's goods" does not describe wealth. The phrase refers primarily to two things — property and money, at whatever level they may exist in your life.

That includes all of us, doesn't it? You see, there is no use talking about love if it does not relate to our material possessions. And if we cannot share those things with people who are in need, we are light years removed from God's love.

And yet that happens frequently. We wall off our hearts. We know that someone close by has a legitimate need, but we won't respond. We slam the door of our hearts, and we hang on to the stuff that is ours, what we've worked hard for. Maybe you need to think about your role here. What have you provided to someone else in the name of love, with no repayment necessary? Maybe they need time as a couple alone. Have you watched their kids for them? Perhaps they need somebody to talk to. Did you invite them over or take them out to eat? Maybe they've run into some lean times financially. You may not have much, but what about a bag of groceries? Their home is showing signs of wear, they don't have the funds to fix it . . . but you're good with your hands, and it wouldn't take you long.

Edwin Markham understood what we're talking about. He's a poet who died in 1940 . . . 88 years old . . . famous for the poem, "The Man with the Hoe." He also wrote, "How the Great Guest Came." It's the story of a cobbler, a devout Christian, who had a dream. He dreamed Jesus was coming to his shop to see him personally. When he awakened, he was so convinced the dream was real that he started making preparations. He went out and bought the most expensive food he could find to feed Jesus. He decorated the place appropriately to receive the Lord.

That day, an old man, a beggar, came by . . . he was down on his luck. His shoes were completely worn through the soles. The cobbler gave him a good pair of shoes out of the love of his heart. An old woman came by. She had a heavy load; she was tired and hungry. The cobbler took that expensive food he had bought for Jesus and gave some of it to her.

He stepped out into the street, and there was a tearful child who was lost and bewildered. He picked her up—kissed and comforted her—and found out where she lived. It was across town, so he rushed across town, returned the child to her mother and then went back home and waited. Evening came and then darkness. He became sad, and finally cried out:

> "Why is it, Lord, that Your feet delay?
> Did You forget that this was the day?"
> Then soft in the silence a Voice he heard:
> "Lift up your heart, for I kept My word . . .
> I was the beggar with bruised feet;
> I was the woman you gave to eat;
> I was the child on the homeless street."[6]

Too often, in our mad dash to recapture some of the old lunch-bag experiences of life, we miss our own opportunity to fill those lunch bags with meaningful expressions of love, and we end up just blowing in hot air. That's why John adds, "Little children, let us not love with word or with tongue, but in deed and truth" (3:18).

John does not mean that words are unimportant. An encouraging word, a kind word is never out of place. But if our demonstrations of love stop with words, or if our words express an attitude that is not consistent with the heart, then such words are hypocritical. Talk is often the easy way out. Action that demonstrates love is the hard way.

RECEIVE YOUR SACK FROM CHRIST

Now then, let me say one more thing. It might be possible to get the impression that the sum total of Christianity is love for others, and therefore to conclude that anyone who shows love is a Christian. That's not the way John sees it. Before any of God's love can filter from our lives, we must personally and individually have experienced and entered into that love ourselves. Look at verse 23 of chapter 3: "And this is His commandment, that we believe in the name of His Son Jesus Christ, and love one another, just as He commanded us."

To believe in Jesus Christ means to believe the Good News about Jesus—that He is God's Son, that He came to save men and women from their sins, and that by believing in Him they can have eternal life.

Belief in the name of Jesus means believing in the nature and character of Christ. It means to believe that He is the Son of God, that He does stand in relation to God the Father in a way in which no other person in the universe ever stood or ever can stand; that He can perfectly reveal God to men, and that He is the Savior of our souls. To believe in the name of Jesus Christ is to accept Him for who He really is.

Remember Robert Fulghum—the lunch bag? Let's revisit the scene—with some changes. Instead of Molly, we'll think in terms of Jesus Christ. READ ON . . .

"Jesus Christ had given me His treasures. All that a Savior held dear. LOVE IN A PAPER SACK. And I had missed it. Not only missed it, but had thrown it in the wastebasket because there wasn't anything in there I needed." DEAR GOD.

Sometimes I think of all the times in this sweet life when I must have missed the LOVE I was being given. A friend calls this "standing knee deep in the river and dying of thirst." So the worn paper sack is there in the box. Left over from a time when the Savior said, "HERE, THIS IS THE BEST I'VE GOT. SUCH AS I HAVE, GIVE I TO THEE."

I missed it the first time. BUT IT'S MY BAG NOW!

Notes

CHAPTER ONE

1. D.A. Carson, *Showing the Spirit, A Theological Exposition of 1 Corinthians 12–14* (Grand Rapids: Baker Book House, 1987), 61.
2. Gary Inrig, *Quality Friendship* (Chicago: Moody Press, 1981), 147–48.
3. Cited by Leo Buscaglia in *Love* (New York: Fawcett Crest Books, 1972), 96–97.
4. Amy Carmichael, *IF* (Fort Washington, Pennsylvania: Christian Literature Crusade, 1966).
5. John Chrysostom in *Homilies or Hebrews,* cited in *Christianity Today,* 18 April 1986, 14.
6. John Wesley, *Pleasing All Men,* from "Alive Now," March/April 1988.
7. Peter Salovey and Judith Rodin, "The Heart of Jealousy," *Psychology Today,* September 1985, 22.
8. Cited by John Powell, *The Secret of Staying in Love* (Niles, Illinois: Argus Communications, 1974), 44.
9. Lewis B. Smedes, *Caring and Commitment* (San Francisco: Harper Collins Publishers, Inc. 1988), 10–11.
10. Joseph Parker, *The People's Bible* Vol. XXV, Ephesians–Revelation (London and Aylesbury: Hazell, Watson, and Viney Ltd., 1915), 52–55.
11. Margery Williams, *The Velveteen Rabbit* (New York: Doubleday and Company, Inc., 1958), 16–17.

CHAPTER TWO

1. Robert Fulghum, *All I Really Need to Know I Learned in Kindergarten* (New York: Villard Books, 1988), 56–58.
2. Charles R. Swindoll, *The Quest for Character* (Portland, Oregon: Multnomah Press, 1987), 67.
3. John Powell, *The Secret of Staying in Love* (Niles, Illinois: Argus Communications, 1974), 48.
4. William Barclay, *The Letter to the Romans* (Philadelphia: The Westminster Press, 1957), 178.
5. Ben Haden, "Sheep Getting Courage" (Changed Lives, Chattanooga, Tennessee, 1989), 13–14.
6. William Hendricksen, *New Testament Commentary, Exposition of Paul's Epistle to the Romans* (Grand Rapids: Baker Book House, 1981), 415.

7. A.W. Tozer, *Of God and Men* (Harrisburg, Pennsylvania: Christian Publications, 1960), 8, 10.
8. Bruce Larson, *Dare to Live Now* (Grand Rapids: Zondervan Publishing House, 1987), 110.
9. Bruce Thielemann, "Legions of the Unjazzed," 5, from *Preaching Today*, Tape 36.

CHAPTER   THREE

1. "The Scope of Modern Hostility," *Psychology Today*, October 1983, 14.
2. John Steinbeck, *America and Americans* (New York: Viking Press, 1966), 139.
3. Willard Gaylin, *The Rage Within: Anger in Modern Life* (New York: Simon and Schuster, 1984), 129.
4. Leo Buscaglia, *Loving Each Other* (Thorofare, New Jersey: Slack Incorporated, 1984), 67–68.
5. Dwight Hervey Small, *After You've Said I Do* (New York: Pillar, 1976), 106.
6. A.T. Robertson, *Studies in the Epistle of James* (Nashville, Tennessee: Broadman Press n.d.), 63.
7. Theodore Isaac Rubin, *Real Love: What It Is, and How to Find It* (New York: The Continuum Publishing Company, © 1990 by El-Ted Rubin), 177.
8. Walt McCuistion, *Mirror, Mirror on the Wall* (Palo Alto: Discovery Papers, 1983), 1.
9. Redford Williams, "The Trusting Heart," *Psychology Today*, February 1989, 36–42.
10. Clifton Fadiman, *The Little Brown Book of Anecdotes* (Boston: Little, Brown and Company Limited, 1985), 360.
11. McCuistion, 2.
12. Dan Hamilton, *Forgiveness* (Downers Grove, Illinois: InterVarsity Press, 1980), 6.
13. William Barclay, *The Daily Study Bible, The Letters of James and Peter* (Toronto: G.R. Welsh Co., Ltd., 1976), 58.
14. Fred B. Craddock, "Who Cares?" from *Preaching Today*, tape #17.

CHAPTER   FOUR

1. Clifton Fadiman, *The Little Brown Book of Anecdotes* (Boston: Little, Brown and Company, 1985), 425.
2. Leo Buscaglia, *Loving Each Other* (Thorofare, New Jersey: Slack Incorporated, 1984), 121.
3. Lloyd John Ogilvie, *Discovering God's Will in Your Life* (Harvest House Publishers, 1982), 41.
4. Theodore Isaac Rubin, *Real Love: What It Is, and How to Find It* (New York: The Continuum Publishing Company, © 1990 by El-Ted Rubin), 72, 104–05.
5. Sydney J. Harris, *The Best of Sydney J. Harris* (Boston: Houghton Mifflin Company, 1976), 101–02.

6. Rubin, 28.
7. John Blanchard, *Truth for Life* (High Street, Welwyn, Hertforshire, England, 1986), 209.
8. Max Lucado, *The Applause of Heaven* (Dallas: Word Publishing, 1990), 107–08.

CHAPTER FIVE

1. Lewis B. Smedes, *Forgive and Forget: Healing the Hurts We Don't Deserve* (San Francisco: Harper Collins Publishers, Inc., 1984), xii–xv.
2. R.V.G. Tasker, *The Gospel According to Matthew* (Grand Rapids: William B. Eerdmans Publishing Co., 1983), 173–74.
3. Abigail Van Buren, "When Your Husband Is Unfaithful," *McCalls* (January 1963), 74.
4. David W. Augsburger, *Cherishable: Love and Marriage* (Scottsdale, Pennsylvania: Herald Press, 1971), 141–42.
5. Max Lucado, *God Came Near* (Portland, Oregon: Multnomah Press, 1987), 101–05.
6. Gail and Gordon MacDonald, *If Those Who Reach Could Touch* (Old Tappan, New Jersey: Fleming H. Revell Co., 1984), 92.
7. Ann Weems, "The Treasure," cited in *Parables, Etc.*, December 1986, 5/6.10.5.
8. Lewis B. Smedes, *Caring and Commitment* (San Francisco: Harper Collins Publishers, Inc., 1988), 121.

CHAPTER SIX

1. Paul Brand and Philip Yancey, *In His Image* (Grand Rapids: Zondervan Publishing House, 1984), 197, 199.
2. John Naisbitt, *Megatrends* (New York: Warner Books, 1982), 150.
3. Martin Luther, *A Commentary on St. Paul's Epistle to the Galatians* (Cambridge and London: James Clarke and Co., Ltd., 1972), 538.
4. Susannah Spurgeon and Joseph Harrold, *C.H. Spurgeon Autobiography* (Carlisle, Pennsylvania: The Banner of Truth Trust, Vol. 1, 1985), 24.
5. Author unknown.
6. Cited by Zig Ziglar in *Top Performance* (Old Tappan, New Jersey: Fleming H. Revell Co., 1986), 44.
7. John R.W. Stott, *Only One Way, The Message of Galatians* (London, England: InterVarsity Press, 1973), 162.
8. Dale E. Galloway, *Dream a New Dream* (Wheaton, Illinois: Tyndale House Publishers, Inc., 1975), 77–78.

CHAPTER SEVEN

1. Richard Selzer, *Letters to a Young Doctor* (New York: Simon and Schuster, Inc., 1982), 143–46.
2. Margaret N. Barnhouse, *That Man Barnhouse* (Wheaton, Illinois: Tyndale House Publishers, Inc., 1985), 110–11.
3. James Wagenvoord (editor), *Men: A Book for Women* (Copyright 1978 by

Product Development International Holding, n.v. Reprinted by permission of Avon Books, New York).

4. Theodore Isaac Rubin, *Real Love: What It Is, and How to Find It* (New York: The Continuum Publishing Company, © 1990 by El-Ted Rubin), 156–57.

5. Richard C. Halverson, *No Greater Power* (Portland, Oregon: Multnomah Press, 1986), 114.

6. Amy Carmichael, cited by Jay Strack in *Shake Off the Dust* (Nashville, Tennessee: Thomas Nelson Publishing, 1988), 164.

7. Ted Brooks, "Something for His File."

CHAPTER EIGHT

1. David Niven, *The Oxford Book of Military Anecdotes*, Max Hastings, Editor (New York: Oxford University Press, 1985), 468–69.

2. M. Scott Peck, *People of the Lie* (New York: Simon and Schuster, 1983), 221.

3. R. Kent Hughes, "The Heart That Ministers (John 4:1-9)" (Wheaton, Illinois: College Church of Wheaton, 17 February 1980), No. 12.

4. Theodore Isaac Rubin, *Real Love: What It Is, and How to Find It* (New York: The Continuum Publishing Company, © 1990 by El-Ted Rubin), 80.

5. Gary Inrig, *A Call to Excellence* (Wheaton, Illinois: Victor Books, 1985), 39.

6. Charles Colson, *Loving God* (Grand Rapids: Zondervan Publishing House, 1983), 127.

7. Adapted from Robert N. Bellah, Richard Madsen, William M. Sullivan, Ann Swidler and Steven M. Tipton, *Habits of the Heart* (Berkeley and Los Angeles, California: University of California Press, 1985), 77.

8. Pierre Mornell, *Passive Men, Wild Women* (New York: Ballantine Books, 1980), 116.

9. Allan Bloom, *The Closing of the American Mind* (New York: Simon and Schuster, 1987), 141.

10. Richard C. Halverson, *No Greater Power* (Portland, Oregon: Multnomah Press, 1986), 74–75.

11. Bruce Larson, *There's a Lot More to Health Than Not Being Sick* (Waco, Texas: Word Books Publishing, 1981), 104.

12. Robert Fulghum, *All I Really Need to Know I Learned in Kindergarten*, (New York: Villard Books, 1988) 78–80.

13. Ruth Harms Calkins, *Lord, Don't You Love Me Anymore?* (Wheaton, Illinois: Tyndale House Publishers, Inc., 1988), 11–12.

CHAPTER NINE

1. Charles R. Swindoll, *Strengthening Your Grip* (Waco, Texas: Word Books, 1982), 65–66.

2. John White and Ken Blue, *Healing the Wounded* (Downers Grove, Illinois: InterVarsity Press, 1985), 54–55.

3. Adapted from Dean Merrill, "After the Fiasco: Restoring Fallen Christians," *Leadership*, Fall 1983, Vol. IV, No. 4 (Christianity Today, Inc., Carol Stream, Illinois), 59–60.

4. Anne Ortlund, *Love Me with Tough Love* (Waco, Texas: Word Books, 1979), 141.
5. Haddon Robinson, "On Target," in *Focal Point,* published by Denver Seminary, 1–2.
6. Ben Haden, "Hope Exception" (from Changed Lives, Chattanooga, Tennessee), 13–14.
7. Paul Benware, "Mind Your Own Business" *(Moody Monthly,* September 1984), 26–27.
8. G. Campbell Morgan, *The Westminster Pulpit* (Grand Rapids: Baker Book House, 1954–1955), Vol. 5, 231–32.
9. Cited by R. Kent Hughes, "Assaulting the Castle Dark," sermon on Acts 19:8-20 (College Church of Wheaton, Wheaton, Illinois, 8 August 1982), 7.

C H A P T E R   T E N

1. Judith Viorst, *I'll Fix Anthony* (cited in *Leadership,* Spring 1986, Vol. VII, Number 2), 46.
2. Lofton Hudson, *Grace Is Not a Blue-Eyed Blond* (Waco, Texas: Word Books, 1972), 93.
3. Theodore Isaac Rubin, *Real Love: What It Is, and How to Find It* (New York: The Continuum Publishing Company, © 1990 by El-Ted Rubin), 160.
4. M. Scott Peck, *The Road Less Traveled* (New York: Touchstone Books, Simon and Schuster, 1978), 88.
5. Grace Noll Crowell,"To One in Sorrow."
6. Leo Buscaglia, *Loving Each Other* (Thorofare, New Jersey: SLACK Incorporated, 1984), 96.
7. John Calvin, *Commentaries on the Epistle of Paul the Apostle to the Romans,* translated and edited by the Rev. John Owen (Grand Rapids: Wm. B. Eerdmans Publishing Company, 1959), 471–72.
8. Charles R. Swindoll, "Consistency," *Think It Over,* Church Newsletter (Fullerton, California: First Evangelical Free Church, n.d.).
9. Howard Hendricks, cited in *Leadership* (Spring 1984, Vol. 5, No. 2), 31.
10. Reprinted with permission from *Guideposts* Magazine. Copyright 1972, Guideposts Associates, Inc., Carmel, New York 10512.

C H A P T E R   E L E V E N

1. Charles R. Swindoll, *Dropping Your Guard* (Waco, Texas: Word Books Publishers, 1983), 115–16.
2. Willard Gaylin, *The Rage Within — Anger in Modern Life* (New York: Simon and Schuster, 1984), 29.
3. William Glasser, *Reality Therapy: A New Approach to Psychiatry* (New York: Harper and Row, 1975), 9.
4. Cited by C.E.B. Cranfield in *A Critical and Exegetical Commentary on the Epistle to the Romans* (Edinburgh: T&T Clark Ltd., 1981), Vol. 2, 674.
5. Theodore Isaac Rubin, *Real Love: What It Is, and How to Find It* (New York: The Continuum Publishing Company, © 1990 by El-Ted Rubin), 187.

6. Charles G. Finney in *Principles of Love* edited by Louis Gifford Parkhurst, Jr. as cited in *Christianity Today*, 3 April 1987.

7. Cited by Barbara Johnson in *Fresh Elastic for Stretched Out Moms* (Old Tappan, New Jersey: Fleming H. Revell Co., 1986), 169–71.

8. Cited by Cranfield, 678, note 2.

9. Cited in *Preaching*, September/October 1988 (Preaching Resources, Inc., 1529 Cesery Blvd., Jacksonville, Florida), 60.

10. William Glasser, *Take Effective Control of Your Life* (New York: Harper and Row Publishers, 1984), 128.

11. Fritz Rienecker, *A Linguistic Key to the Greek New Testament* (Grand Rapids: Regency Reference Library, Zondervan Publishing House, 1980), 379.

12. Billy Graham, "What the Bible Says About Sex," *The Marriage Affair*, J. Allan Petersen, ed. (Wheaton, Illinois: Tyndale House Publishers, Inc., 1971), 370.

13. Ray Stedman, *Expository Studies in Romans 9–16, From Guilt to Glory*, Vol. II (Waco, Texas: Word Books Publisher, 1978), 136.

14. Written by Nancy L. Dahlberg, reported in *The Pastor's Story File*, December 1985 (Saratoga Press, P.O. Box 8, 313 Elizabeth Ave., Platteville, Colorado 80651-0008, 303-785-2990), 2–3.

CHAPTER TWELVE

1. Robert Fulghum, *It Was on Fire When I Lay On It* (New York: Villard Books, 1989), 27–31.

2. Joseph R. Cooke, *Free for the Taking* (Old Tappan, New Jersey: Fleming H. Revell, 1975), 29.

3. Theodore Isaac Rubin, *Real Love: What It Is, and How to Find It* (New York: The Continuum Publishing Company, © 1990 by El-Ted Rubin), 198.

4. Lewis B. Smedes, *Forgive and Forget: Healing the Hurts We Don't Deserve* (San Francisco: Harper Collins Publishers, Inc., 1984), 20.

5. Richard Selzer, *Mortal Lessons: Notes in the Art of Surgery* (New York: Simon and Schuster, 1976), 45–46.

6. Edwin Markham, "How the Great Guest Came."